BILLION DOLLAR SALES

SECRETS

BILLION DOLLAR SALES

SECRETS

,,,

SUPERSTAR SELLING TIPS

FOR ALL SEASONS

JOE PARANTEAU

ISBN 978-1-7352327-7-5 (hardcover)
ISBN 978-1-7352327-5-1 (paperback)
ISBN 978-1-7352327-0-6 (ebook)

Library of Congress Control Number 2020922989

Permission to use material from other works.

Cover and interior design by G Sharp Design, LLC.
Contributions and editing by Andy Earle.

Printed in the United States of America.
Published by Joseph Paranteau, Dallas, TX

For permission requests or bulk orders, please visit billiondollarsalessecrets.com.

"To all the advisors, coaches, and mentors who have helped me grow into the person I am today. And to my family. I am forever grateful."

CONTENTS

INTRODUCTION

Thank you for purchasing this book! I hope you gain value from the insights I learned as a professional salesperson for 30 years. Years ago, I set a goal for myself: I wanted to sell more than a billion dollars in revenue. I had the opportunity to have substantial annual sales quotas (ranging from $20M-$300M) and work with thousands of customers. In less than five years, I surpassed my billion-dollar goal. As I wrote this book, my employer became the world's most valuable company with a market capitalization of 1.1 trillion dollars. But my time at working in big tech is only part of my story. I have another two decades of experience working in startups and coaching salespeople, in addition to the skills I gained serving in the military.

Over the years, I've had peers, mentors, and customers beg me to share the insights I gained from thousands of interactions and experiences. I picture readers of this book ranging from seasoned veterans to first time sellers. For the experienced salesperson, there may be some tips you never considered; hopefully, you will gain some new perspectives. For new salespeople, this will help you build good habits and work from the inside out as you develop skills and knowledge. In this book, you'll learn proven principles to help you answer questions like:

- What's preventing me from succeeding in sales?

- How do I get started in sales?

- How do I advance a sale?

- How should I structure my sales calls to reach my desired outcomes?

- How do I stand out from the crowd?

- How do I manage my business, boss, and partnerships to reach a common goal?

- What can I expect if I am successful?

These sales secrets make up my "little black book" full of specific information I've used countless times in my career. You'll discover in-the-trenches street smarts, basic sales lessons, training tips, and scientific research in this book. My unique selling career is grounded in Human & Organizational Communication, Psychology, Sociology, Business, and Engineering. I used to sell to sellers, which helped me get real good at selling. I've had formal training in many modern sales methodologies, plus a wealth of personal experiences gained from living in many different places and cultures. I've had many kinds of sales experiences, including 10+ years in direct marketing, professional business-to-business (B2B) sales, owning small businesses, volunteering, and door-to-door selling.

My secrets have been tested and proven in ways such as:

- Outmaneuvering competitors to win multi-million dollar, multi-year complex B2B sales

- Satisfying customers and growing businesses

➤ Growing a direct marketing business from the ground up to be a valuable passive income stream

➤ Growing a small business customer base and market presence

➤ Buying and negotiating complex real estate deals

Here's your first free sales secret – the enemy of sales is TIME! Don't stop reading after the introduction or just cherry-pick the chapters that seem interesting. Create your action plan now. Invest your time and dive in. What are you waiting for?

LOOK INSIDE

6,500 feet in the air and hours into my first cross-country solo flight, I hit a patch of gut-wrenching turbulence that shook me to my core and made me realize that I was standing in the way of my success. My gas gauge was bouncing all over the place. Suddenly my mind thought I was losing fuel. I started to hyperventilate, my skin got clammy, and sweat dripped down my forehead. My eyesight dimmed, and then I remembered what my instructor told me: "relax, breathe deeply, fly the plane." I did precisely that, and when I was out of the turbulence, my fuel gauges stabilized. I had not yet studied this, but fuel gauges work by floats in the tank that are disrupted by turbulence. I learned not to trust the gauges in the plane for fuel. Fuel is time, so I watched the clock like a hawk. Alone, thousands of feet in the air, I almost sabotaged myself by panicking. I needed to do some work on myself.

And so do you.

You're probably not flying a plane, but you need to have total mastery over yourself and learn how to better yourself to succeed genuinely. In this chapter, you'll learn to find your brand, challenge your biases, and set your intentions.

The first secret to taking your sales performance to new levels is understanding your weaknesses and seeking to improve them. You have to lose your baggage to work more complex deals. Introspection will strengthen your hustle. In this chapter, you will receive exercises and tools for discovering your motivations behind selling, your strengths and weaknesses, and how to take control of your selling career. You'll start by taking stock of who you are because your brand is your biggest asset as a seller. Then I'll show you how to shift your attention from your past to your future so you can get rid of your biases. But removing biases is only half the battle; you have to go one step further and learn how to set your intentions, find your reason to care about what you're selling, and orient yourself towards others. This chapter will cover that and conclude with a few concrete tips for improving yourself personally and professionally.

You may doubt a book can change your selling career, and that's why we start with *you*. Change comes from within, and you need to focus on your mindset to lay the foundations for lasting change. The right mindset will serve as a significant asset throughout your career. You want to stay introspective and in tune with your ambitions. The secrets in this book will give you many tools for success, but in the end, you are the one who has to act. If you are a student of growth and self-improvement, you are well suited to a successful career. Selling will return dividends in all areas of your life, but you must know yourself well to sell well. Maybe you aren't used to taking a long, hard look at yourself and don't know where to begin. Objectively taking stock of your assets, weaknesses, and biases is challenging, especially if you don't like what you find. While looking inside isn't so simple, this chapter will help you get there one step at a time.

LET'S START WITH YOUR STORY — WHY ARE YOU SELLING?

The first phase of looking inside yourself is to get your story straight. Check yourself at the door and get real. If you don't have a firm grasp of your own story, you won't be able to communicate what makes you unique and why customers should buy from you. Having a clearly articulated story for yourself will remind you why you love selling when business gets tough. Ask yourself questions like "How did I get into selling?" and "Why do I want to sell?" Maybe you're deliberate, or perhaps you're like me and started your sales career somewhat by accident. Answering these questions will get your journey of introspection started. Going back to the beginning of your sales career can help you understand why you chose this path. The following self-assessment will open you to more reflection and get you thinking deeply about yourself as a salesperson.

Over the next few pages, I'm going to walk you through tools that will help you explore your history and motivations. Look at your personal history, unique experiences, and baggage. Embrace *your* story and *your* motivations for selling; these will be assets that help you create your ideal future. You'll want to unpack and wrestle with these before we dive into selling any further. Are you ready to take this journey together?

Self-Assessment

Examine your experiences, goals, dreams, and current situation. Take a moment and answer these questions right now. Don't gloss over this! You may think you know yourself well, but self-knowledge is the foundation for success, so don't move forward until you are sure.

1. Why do you want to sell?

2. How will you help people get what they want or need?

3. What preconceived notions do you have that are creating barriers to your future success?

4. What will happen if you don't make a change right here, right now? What does the path of inaction look like?

5. Picture yourself as a successful salesperson. What does your life look like? What images come to mind? What will it allow you to do? Be very descriptive.

6. Who are the people in your life you will invest in? These are people you know and love whom you are going to help.

7. Identify the people in your life that will help you. Whom do you need, and why? Even if no one specific comes to mind, what kind of people do you need?

Answer these questions now, and then reflect on them again after you've finished the book. Introspection is an ongoing journey; you're constantly changing, so you need to check in with yourself consistently! Speaking of change, let's talk about how your past relates to your present – and ultimately your future.

FIND YOUR FUEL

The second step in preparing yourself to change your altitude is to discover what motivates you. It's easy to lose motivation as a seller, especially in bad economies or with demanding clients. If you lose your motivation, your numbers will drop, and that can jeopardize the momentum you've built over your career, so it's critical to zero in on your motivations. You'll be surprised how helpful this can be.

Anytime you find yourself frustrated or overwhelmed, remember why you chose this career in the first place.

Reflecting on your motivations will make your work more meaningful. You may worry that the path to your dreams is impossible. But even if you're living in a blue-collar town, that doesn't mean you can't become a CEO one day. Your past doesn't define you. In fact, it can inspire you.

I'm an example of this, as I draw motivation from my upbringing. I grew up in poverty, fantasizing daily about future success. I'm Native American and Métis, meaning I'm both American Indian and Canadian, and I'm the first generation in my family to grow up "off the rez." My dad was born in Harlem, Montana, on the Ft. Belknap Indian Reservation, and grew up in a house with a dirt floor and wooden slats for walls. He escaped Montana's cold through military service and met my mother, but they divorced when I was young. Growing up, we never had any money. My brother, sister, and I would paint rocks and go door-to-door, selling them as paperweights. I was the salesperson, and my brother was the artist. My sister made sure no one ripped us off. I think many of those early sales were due to our neighbor's charity. We were always struggling, getting our power disconnected, and shopping at scratch-and-dent grocery stores or thrift stores. Instead of getting new pants, we'd patch up old ones or go dumpster diving. I envied those who had more than us, and it's what fueled me to break the cycle of poverty. Wanting more is a powerful emotion, and it can be a strong motivator.

So, what's fueling you forward? Having a chip on your shoulder isn't a bad thing if it propels you instead of holding you back. Michael Jordan had a chip on his shoulder because his high school coach didn't see his greatness. So did Walt Disney, who was labeled "not creative."

Too many people believe their present situation defines their future. The fact is that where you are now doesn't matter. Going forward, *you* choose to either be the victim or the victor.

If you're at the same point where you were five years ago, ask yourself if you're growing. How much value are you adding to other people and the marketplace? If you are stagnant, why? Maybe you've accepted where you are and stopped dreaming. Perhaps you have rationalized mediocrity or even defeat. I don't claim to know your situation, but if you believe you can do more, you can. You and I are just getting started on an incredible ride together. You want to learn more about selling, and I want to share some great lessons with you. But the story begins and ends with you. Change happens from the inside out.

DROP PRECONCEIVED NOTIONS

With your story and motivations in mind, the next step is to take stock of what biases and preconceived notions you might be harboring. Unfounded biases will only hold you back and make you a less successful salesperson. Identify and let go of these to free yourself up for more sales. It's unlikely you've gone through life without acquiring unfair biases based on negative experiences, and you need to challenge yourself to think about these. There are many unconscious bias tests you can take online to understand beliefs you may not know you hold. You should also reflect on the first impression you tend to have upon meeting someone new. Did you automatically assume the car salesman was sleazy? Did you think the young customer would be naive and easier to sell to?

I learned the importance of invisible biases while working in college for a major stock brokerage making cold calls to retirement communities to drive attendance for upcoming investment events. I didn't like rejection. It's hard not to take rejection personally, especially when you're only spending a few minutes on the phone with people. But I learned that if you called 100 people, you could count on a few positive calls out of the bunch; you're always only a call away from someone saying yes. It's the law of averages – if you make enough calls, you still get a few good ones. On average, every 100 dials would net 8-10 interested people, and I learned to hope for the best instead of expecting the worst. Dropping my negative bias that the calls would go poorly helped improve my sales.

If I opened the call with a bad attitude, expecting rejection, I was likely to come across as unenthusiastic and insincere. But when I told myself the call would be great, I was in a better mood, and the customer could tell. A popular saying for salespeople making cold calls is, "Have the enthusiasm of a golden retriever, and the memory of a goldfish." Forget the sales you don't make, and stay positive.

If you want to be successful in sales, you must open yourself to new ways of thinking. Be open to watching, listening, and learning as much as possible while preparing to implement what you've learned through immediate action. If you go into sales with a fixed mindset, you'll have trouble connecting with potential customers. I'm asking you to challenge and drop your preconceived notions: if you go into a pitch assuming the client will say "No" based on some unfounded bias, it's unlikely you'll make the sale. If you are new to selling, you need to be open and honest when identifying your weak spots.

What preconceived notions do you have that may get in the way of your success in sales and life? Are you open to challenging yourself and growing? Managing your beliefs and biases is crucial to true self-discovery. Now, let's talk about choosing the right thoughts.

SET YOUR INTENTIONS

After dropping your biases, focus your thoughts, and set your intentions. If you're not intentional in your choices and don't allocate your effort and resources properly, you'll spread yourself thin. You can have a million great ideas, but if you can't focus your attention and energy on one, you'll end up with a dozen half-fulfilled dreams.

When you lack focus, you inevitably fail to follow through. Ask yourself questions like "Do I have many partially completed tasks?" and "Do I tend to take on multiple new projects and then abandon them?" People who lack focus are full of ideas but ultimately fall short of their goals because they give 10% to 10 different ambitions instead of 100% to one dream. That's why it's time to focus up.

You probably have many lofty ambitions and a wealth of ideas for your career. Maybe you're an entrepreneur and have multiple projects you're pursuing. Or perhaps you aren't sure about your direction. Either way, it's time to focus your mind on one primary goal and dedicate yourself to achieving it. You have many choices to make every day, the most powerful of which is what to think about. Your life may not be what you want it to be right now, and that's okay. Decide what you want to work towards and focus your thoughts and energy on that goal. Focused attention is more effective than haphazard wishing.

Great thinkers throughout the ages have highlighted the relationship between thought and destiny. Lou Tice, the Pacific Institute founder, said, "We move toward and become what we think about."[1] Our thoughts are potent. They shape our lives. Steven Covey popularized this in his book *The 7 Habits of Highly Effective People* when he shared, "Sow a thought, reap an action; sow an action, reap a habit;

---

1   Pacific Institute. (n.d.). Retrieved 2 3, 2019, from Pacific Institute: http://www.pacinst.org

sow a habit, reap a character; sow a character, reap a destiny."[2]

In the Bible, Jesus says, "The eye is the lamp of the body. If your eyes are good, your whole body will be full of light" (Matthew 6:22).[3] He said this because our eyes are the entrance to our hearts and minds. His warning was to be careful of what you are feeding yourself.

What you consume influences how you think about the world and interact with it. Better yourself by being intentional with the media you consume and the thoughts you entertain. How often do you think about what you are feeding yourself?

One way our thoughts may be pulled in a negative direction is through the overuse of social media. I'm not saying dump social media or TV completely but choose carefully which types of media you consume. Don't let the media dictate what you think about, but focus your thoughts on bettering yourself. Recent evidence suggests a connection between social media and depression. Dr. Jeff Nalin, a respected leader in clinical psychology and dependence issues, notes the choices teens make with social media can lead to isolation, decreased social skills, and cyberbullying.[4] And it's not just teens: there is ample evidence adults are affected by these vices too. Social media is a growing cause of relationship dissatisfaction. We lose control of our thoughts in a world of text strings, sound bites, and video clips. How do you choose what to focus on?

The idea that you move toward what you think about has influenced me in every area of my life. I often picture myself being suc-

2   Covey, Stephen R. *The 7 Habits of Highly Effective People: Powerful Lessons in Personal Change.* New York: Simon & Schuster, 2004.

3   Zondervan Publishing, Life Application Study Bible: New International Version, Black, Top Grain Leather (2005)

4   "Social Media and Teen Depression: The Two Go Hand-In-Hand," Anxiety and Depression Association of America, ADAA, accessed November 8, 2020, https://adaa.org/learn-from-us/from-the-experts/blog-posts/consumer/social-media-and-teen-depression-two-go-hand.

cessful in my mind before I achieve my goals. I've learned to be a voracious reader and consumer of information. I'd feed myself motivational stories to keep my energy up. We all love those stories, except most of us haven't written our own yet! Let's break down the steps to find, follow, and focus your intentions:

1. **Start with big dreams** – The first step to setting your intentions and focusing your thoughts is to dream big. Make your masterpiece, and don't talk yourself into something less than a big, bold, crazy vision. I don't care what people say about making it practical; life isn't practical. How many people are truly living their dreams?

2. **Set goals** – Once you've got dreams, the next step is translating them into goals. Goals are dreams with deadlines. You need to break down your dreams and figure out how to get there. Create SMART goals, meaning they are specific, measurable, achievable, realistic, and time-bound.

3. **Find models** – Next, find people who have done what you want to do and talk to them so you can emulate their path to success. If no one has done it, find people who were trailblazers in similar areas. You can learn a lot from what others have done to achieve success and by relentlessly reading books, listening to podcasts, watching videos, and interviewing others about their success.

4. **Develop habits** – The final step in setting your intentions is to learn the patterns of behavior that led your models to succeed. In developing your habits, you will want to identify what explicit actions you need to take and when. Change isn't easy, but you're on the right track if you have the right

habits. It generally takes about 21 days of consistency to develop a new habit, and once you have it down, it seems effortless. If you have good habits, over time, they yield success.

Use these steps to guide your thoughts and habits, and start envisioning the success you want!

FIND A REASON TO CARE

After setting your intentions, it's time to get passionate and find something that lights your fire. Before you can inspire customers to care about your product, you have to care for yourself. This chapter is all about *you*, and learning to care about what you're selling is crucial to your success. We've talked about finding your story, your motivation, and your fuel for selling. Reflecting on these should uncover how and why you care!

What moves you? Why do you want to sell this? Asking yourself these questions will make you a better salesperson and prepare you for any pushback from potential customers. Maybe you care because you know your product saves lives, or you might overlook it because you love your company and want to support it. Perhaps you care because you are committed to providing a good life for your family. Whatever your reason, channel this passion and energy into your sales. This is important because when you care about your selling, your enthusiasm rubs off on your clients.

I saw how passion could move people when working as a telemarketer during college for the AIDS Project Los Angeles (APLA). In the early 1990s, AIDS as a disease was not well understood, and it had considerable stigmas attached to it. While the charity I was working with offered compelling benefits to people suffering from terminal illnesses, getting people to care about others over the phone and donate was a challenge. Since I only had a few seconds to engage people, one of the first questions I would ask was, "What are your thoughts about the AIDS crisis?" I learned to pause and not say anything until they answered me. It caught people off guard, so when they responded with "who is this?" I'd ask the question again a little differently, followed by "What do you think YOU CAN DO about the AIDS crisis?" I discarded the script given to me after I encountered hostility when I used it; the challenge of engaging people in different ways was a motivator for me. How could I engage prospective donors in a discussion when most of my peers were getting hung up on? I was emotionally invested in helping people with AIDS, so I wasn't about to give up.

Through my questioning, I got people to open up and ask them more about their opinions by saying "Interesting" or "Really?" I could dive more in-depth to identify times when they needed help, like changing a tire or finding a lost dog. Finally, I'd ask, "Imagine if you could help these people right now with their greatest needs. How would that make you feel?" Almost everyone could empathize with helping another human being, especially after reflecting on times they needed help. I was surprised when people would say to me, "Yes, I want to give $1,000," out of the blue. Most people gave $10-25, but I rarely asked them to do it. People have to give a damn before they are willing to part with their money.

Caring about what you're selling is a crucial motivator. The valuable lesson I learned is that you can't fake it. People can see right through you, even over the phone. If you're genuine about what you're selling, people tend to respond positively. It's contagious, attractive, and moves people to action. I can't recall any of the other businesses or charities I telemarketed for. None gave me the satisfaction of my

APLA discussions. If you don't believe in what you are selling, you can come across as inauthentic. As you read on, do a gut check and ask yourself if you stand behind what you are trying to sell. If it doesn't move you, it likely won't move anyone else.

ORIENT YOURSELF TOWARDS OTHERS

Sales is inherently a people-focused career, so it's crucial you orient yourself to your clients' needs and desires. You've spent the past few pages reflecting on what makes you tick. Now it's time to use your improved understanding of yourself to help others. One of my first sales experiences underlined this vital lesson for me and helped me realize that sales is about using your strengths to help others get what they need.

After college, I interviewed for a sales job, needing to pay off my student loans. A growing company called Software Spectrum partnered with all the major players in technology as a reseller. The reason they were interested in me was not because of any technical knowledge I had; they were interested in my *passion* for technology and my ability to explain it to customers who lacked a technical perspective.

I was fortunate to have a stellar sales leader named Lorraine interview me. I was honest with her that I didn't know much about sales and wasn't thrilled about being a salesperson. I told her I didn't want to con people into something they didn't need and let her know I grew up believing many sleazy stereotypes about salespeople. I needed the money, but I felt bothered about the concept of becoming a salesperson. Was this the professional identity I envisioned for myself? Could I stomach working in sales? Instead of making a judgment, Lorraine explained what professional salespeople do. She said salespeople help customers get what they want. She elaborated that if you're not helping people, you're not selling. Her words changed my understanding of sales and transformed it into a career I felt well-suited for. It sounded different from what I expected, so I said, "This sounds amazing. I want to sell for this company!" My enthusiasm landed me the job, and I continued to learn from Lorraine. She may not know it, but she's a big reason why I wanted to pay it forward with this book.

In those early days, I'd come home each night following sales training and ask, "Did I help someone today?" Then, each morning before I'd go to work, I asserted, "I'm going to help someone today." Reflecting on what I am doing to help others is a habit I continue to do today. It may seem understated, but if you don't believe you can help others, you will never be great in sales.

Not only is sales about helping others, but it is also fundamentally about connecting. Going the extra mile to learn about your clients will set you apart from your competitors. I saw the importance of making that connection at my telemarketing job in college. Through trial and error, I learned to develop rapport and create a relationship with the person on the other end of the line.

To give me a leg up, I studied the etymology of names as a way to build small talk. I could soon strike up a conversation based on the history of various names, including German, Polish, Korean, Kenyan, Irish, and many others. I also learned a lot about the geography of Hemet, Palm Springs, and the Palm Desert in California, where my client base lived. I knew what stores and activities were popular in the area and where the VFW, hospital, and cemetery were located. I used all that information to build rapport in a few seconds over the phone. I took the extra time to find information that would allow me to connect with my clients to foster more authentic conversations and improve my sales.

This chapter has helped you learn more about yourself and how to use that information to help and connect with others. Now for some practical implications...

IMPROVING YOURSELF

Before wrapping up this first chapter, I want to leave you with some tips for applying these self-improvement ideas to your life. We've talked about looking inside and taking stock of yourself, so hopefully, you've followed along with the exercises and are feeling more in tune with your strengths and weaknesses. You should have a better understanding of yourself by now, but you may still be harboring bad habits. All the self-reflection in the world is useless if you don't use it to improve yourself. Here are a few concrete ways to make yourself the best seller you can be.

Don't Be A Jerk

The first self-improvement tip is simple: Don't be a jerk! To take it one step further, be *actively kind and helpful* to others. How you treat others is essential. It says a lot about your character, so if you want to work on your likeability and people skills, both integral to effective selling, show respect and generosity to everyone around you. I experienced this while working for a luxury retailer in their stock room in 1985. I was at the bottom of the corporate hierarchy and doing menial tasks, but I discovered the value of being nice to everyone.

Many of the other employees I interacted with there would talk down to anyone in a lower position. When they were on the sales floor, they were all smiles, elegant, refined, and polished. When they breached the stockroom threshold, they were rude, demeaning, demanding, and pompous. They might have thought their mean outbursts didn't cost them any sales since the customers didn't see, but their negative language was losing them sales, sometimes worth hundreds of dollars per day!

During busy times, like annual sales or the holidays, all hands on deck and stockroom workers like me were on the floor looking as presentable as the sales staff. When the store was busy, it was impossible not to sell. Customers would ask me, "Can you ring me up?" or "Can you help me decide what tie is right for my husband?" The answer was always, "Yes." However, I was an hourly employee, and the salespeople were selling on commission. So I'd always key in the deal for the people who were nicest to me.

I noticed that the salespeople who were nicest to me were also kindest to the customers. Not only was I giving them credit for my sales, but customers were giving them credit for purchases, too. The kindest salespeople had many repeat customers who asked for them by name. They were rock stars! Basic human kindness goes a long way; in addition to being the decent thing to do, being nice to everyone will help your sales.

Get Your Butt Out of Bed

The second self-development tip is to control your sleep schedule: get out of bed early in the morning and call it a day at a reasonable hour each night. Think about your daily routine: when do you wake up and when do you go to bed? If you aren't a morning person already, it's time to become one. Morning is when distractions are minimal, and that's why successful people all wake up early.

When I was in boot camp in the military, I had to wake up earlier than ever. We woke at 4 am, got dressed in 190 seconds flat, and marched off to the mess hall. At the time, I didn't realize the military was training us for success. Your brain is operating at a heightened activity level in the early morning, so why not take advantage of your body's biological activity and make it work for you? Use this extra energy to increase your productivity and creative thinking. Staying up late and delaying sleep until the last minute deprives you of the rest your body needs for recovery and rebuilding.

Here's another way to look at it: You are more finely tuned than a sports car. But your body pushes back when you don't take care of yourself. Your adrenal glands produce cortisol, known as the "stress hormone." Cortisol regulates blood sugar and blood pressure and manages inflammation in the body. Cortisol levels change throughout the day, but they are highest in the morning and lowest at night. Between 10:00 pm and 1:00 am, the adrenal glands are doing repair work. If you don't go to bed early, your adrenal glands will kick in and start producing more cortisol in a "second wind" pattern. This means your adrenal system isn't repairing itself, potentially decreasing your ability to perform well. Your melatonin levels also rise after 9:00 pm or 10:00 pm, a pattern designed to induce drowsiness. The production of melatonin is directly tied to the circadian sunrise-sunset cycle, so you create an imbalance when you stay awake.[5]

Furthermore, your brain waves also change with the time of day; in the morning, you're between theta and alpha brainwave activity—the alpha state bridges both hemispheres of your brain to help you communicate and solve problems better. You are also more creative in this state, and alpha waves release serotonin, which reduces depression and anxiety, heals your body, increases your libido, and improves bone health. Waking up early optimizes your day by keeping you in tune with your body's functions and capitalizing on creative energy. Assess your sleep

5   Javier Labad et al., "The Role of Sleep Quality, Trait Anxiety and Hypothalamic-Pituitary-Adrenal Axis Measures in Cognitive Abilities of Healthy Individuals," *International Journal of Environmental Research and Public Health* 17, no. 20 (2020): xx, doi:10.3390/ijerph17207600.

patterns and make a change if necessary; it'll lead to long-term success.

Breathe, People

The third and final bonus self-development tip is to take control of your breath consciously. I met Tony Horton, creator of the legendary fitness program, P90X, in a group workout. If you've done P90X, you know Tony instructs people to breathe during the workout. It seems like a small thing, but it's foundational. Breathing is one of those things no one ever has to tell you about – it just happens. However, mindfully controlling your breathing is crucial in stressful or high-intensity situations.

Research shows that conscious breathing techniques can help you transition your brain into the alpha state and stabilize your mood.[6] Your diaphragm helps control your mindful breathing, and it's connected directly to your mind by the phrenic nerve. When you breathe for performance, you can control dopamine release and noradrenaline, which helps maintain action, learning, and memory. Breathing will calm you down and put you in a more relaxed, meditative state.

I like to use a specific trick: Take two quick, short inhaled breaths through your nose and one out through your mouth. It's called 2 to 1 breathing, and I learned it in a yoga class taught by Tony Horton. Controlling your breathing will make the difficult parts of your day more manageable. You may not be flying a plane across the country, but your body treats other stress the same way, driving your cortisol levels up. Knowing how to make your body work for you is key. Treat your body right, and it will pay you dividends. As my friend Tony says, "Breathe, people."

---

6   "Mindfulness-of-breathing Exercise Modulates EEG Alpha Activity During Cognitive Performance," Wiley Online Library, last modified June 1, 2016, https://onlinelibrary.wiley.com/doi/abs/10.1111/psyp.12678.

CHAPTER SUMMARY/KEY TAKEAWAYS

In this chapter, you learned:

> **You are the biggest hurdle to your own success**: A weak personal brand, pre-existing biases, and a lack of strong intentions are limiting factors in a sales career.

> **Find your personal brand**: Reflect on your unique story, career path, and motivations for selling to cement your professional identity and communicate to your clients what makes you unique.

> **Confront your biases**: Check your preconceived notions at the door and drop the unfounded prejudices holding you back.

> **Set your intentions**: Focus your energy and attention on one main goal and follow through.

> **Three self-development tips**: Be a student of growth and improvement, continuously developing healthier habits.

> ↪ **Be kind to everyone**: Treat those around you with decency and respect and reap the benefits.

> ↪ **Get up early**: Your body is ready to get started early; capitalize on this natural energy and get going.

> ↪ **Breathe**: Practice 2 to 1 breathing and consciously use your breath to calm yourself.

Now that we are done looking inside, it's time to look at the next piece of the puzzle: The Sale. In the next chapter, you will learn why sales are the lifeblood of any company, as well as the skills and approaches needed for your selling career. Selling is complex and requires you to plan, have a process, and analyze metrics. We're just getting started, so what are you waiting for?

THE YIN AND YANG OF RAPPORT

Building rapport was pivotal early in my career when my employer was vying for a contract to create the first online sales platform for a global airline. Our customer had millions of dollars in travel bookings and operational improvements at stake. While our team had terrific graphic designers, information architects, and technologists, we didn't have all the talent needed to win this deal.

The airline liked our creativity but was worried we couldn't handle the security. Our proposals kept getting rejected. It looked like we were at a standstill. That's when I made the innovative decision to partner with our competitor. With an unlikely team and plan, we won the business, and everyone benefited. Our choice to take this bold, creative approach demonstrates that adaptability can help you effectively connect with customers and land massive sales. Flexibility shows potential clients that you are innovative and eager for their business and is critical to building productive rapport.

One of the best things about selling is connecting with people. If you're thinking, "This is just my job" or "I only care about the money," I hear you. But you probably sound like a robot when you interact with your customers for this very reason. That mindset causes you to be too self-centered. You can spend so much time rehearsing your "pitch" that you fail to invest time in learning about your customers' needs. If you're in B2B sales, learn about the company – how it was started, who the executives are, what their customers think about them, and so on. With direct selling, get to know your customers. Train yourself to sell *with* people, not *to* them.

I went to buy some new clothes and ended up spending far more than I had budgeted because the saleswoman sold *with* me. She asked lots of questions, identified my needs and desires, and focused on how to help me solve my problem. I felt like I had her support, and because I felt like she cared, I was more than willing to part with my money.

To make the sale, you have to build rapport, but connecting with your customers is hard to do. It's challenging to turn a stranger into a customer; it requires nurturing a connection, something not everyone has the social and professional skills to do. You may struggle to pitch to clients who have unrealistic expectations or find it hard to connect with someone in an industry you have little experience in. Maybe your small talk feels forced or fake. In this chapter, I will show you my favorite formula for connecting with customers, but formulas are only half the equation. You also need to be flexible, so in the second half of the chapter, I'll get into adaptability.

FOLLOW A FORMULA

There are many helpful, established approaches to developing a connection with your customer. Many people in network marketing use a technique called FORM, an inquiry-based way to get customers talking. FORM stands for:

> ➤ Family: "Are you married?" or "Do you have kids?"

> ➤ Occupation: "What do you do for a living?"

> ➤ Recreation: "What do you do for fun?"

> ➤ Message: Give your pitch

FORM can be a helpful framework to get other people talking but is also fairly contrived. It's typically useful when trying to recruit others to your direct selling business but won't help you much with B2B sales. Here is my preferred way to approach customers, which works in a variety of contexts. It follows a more easily digestible formula:

GREET-RELATE-QUESTION-REFLECT

Greet

Start with a cheery "Hello" and a warm smile, looking the other person in the eyes directly. Something as simple as "Hi, I'm Joe, what's your name?" works perfectly. If you know their name (or they have a nametag), address them as "Hi Wendy, I'm Joe." Actively listen and focus on your customer to avoid immediately forgetting their name, a rookie mistake. Repetition is a helpful recall trick, so respond with something like, "It's nice to meet you, Wendy," to reinforce your memory.

Relate

Next comes your "relate to" statement or question. What are you going to say to break the ice? Your opening is highly context-dependent, and it needs to feel natural. If you know the client is a local sports fan, share something about a recent game. If they're in finance, bring up a recent article or study. If you know a bit about them in advance, you can read up on relevant topics for small talk, but you have to make it authentic and exciting to connect.

That's why I love using questions to relate to clients. A helpful sales technique involving questioning is called "peeling the onion." As you ask more questions, you discover new layers. Keep the questions situationally relevant. If you know anything about their business, you could ask something like, "I saw the earnings release yesterday, and I was impressed. How has your company been able to wow the market so consistently?" Listen closely to their response to learn about them and discover ways to connect. Here are some other ways to relate to your customer:

➤ Compliment them (e.g., "Love your suit!")

➤ Talk about a shared positive experience. Example: "The weather is so wonderful today!"

➤ Discuss shared hobbies or interests. Example: "Have you had much time to go hiking recently?"

➤ Mention something relevant to their business you saw in the news. For instance, something exciting about their industry or a customer of theirs. Make it quick, intriguing, and upbeat, and stay away from politics. Example: "I think that South America is going to open up a lot for your industry based on what I read in the *Journal*. If you're interested, I can forward the article."

Question

After you greet and relate to your customer, the next step is to pose a question. Be genuine and make it about them. Ask something you actually want to know that will improve your pitch. "How many employees work at this location?" or "How many customers come to visit you here?" If you are in door-to-door sales, set up a clear segue into your pitch. For instance, you might open with "Hi! So, I'm not here today with any winning sweepstakes results, but rather I have some services you might find interesting. How often do you get your windows cleaned?"

I'll never forget one door-to-door salesperson who visited when I was growing up. He came to the door and said: "Hi, I see you have carpet, and I'd like to show you how easy it is to get it clean. Can I show you now?" My carpet was the dirtiest you've ever seen. I got the Kirby vacuum guy all set up, and watched him spray a solution onto the carpet and then suck it up. Holy Cow! Our carpet was a dark beige, not green! He immediately put himself in a situation to demonstrate his product and make a sale by asking a relevant question.

Reflect

The final step is to reflect: take a moment to listen to what the other person is telling you. Instead of focusing on what to say next, make sure you understand them. Follow up by asking clarifying questions, which will improve your knowledge of their business and demonstrate you've been paying attention. Connect with them, process what they tell you, and listen for opportunities to sell.

SALES REQUIRES ADAPTATION

Every client is different, so your formula for connecting might not always work! One day you may find your usual tools aren't working, so you need to practice adapting to any situation. One of the hardest things about building rapport is that different customers have different needs, and these may even change during the course of your relationship. Even if you made an immediate connection, you need to nurture it throughout your relationship as things change. How do you ensure you're presenting the best version of yourself to each customer while keeping up with global changes? It's all about adaptation. You wouldn't sell today the same way someone did in 1920, or even 2019. Trends shift daily, and customers want different things, so you need to develop a growth mindset and become more agile to build rapport with your customers.

You need to be especially flexible when you change industries. I started selling in direct marketing after I'd already achieved success in my B2B career. However, the skills didn't directly translate. I had to go back to school and learn from others. At first, I struggled because I took what made me successful in one situation and tried to apply it somewhere completely different. The opposite is also true: direct marketing gurus often don't succeed in B2B sales at first. While some selling attributes are universal, context is critical. To be a sales leader in your field, you need to study the industry, understand its unique sales context, and find suitable models. For instance, I found that direct marketing is very personal and requires a different approach from B2B sales, focusing more on listening to the customer. Whatever field you are in, you need to adapt your approach to create feelings of connection constantly.

Technology is now playing a critical role in the sales process. Meetings, pitches, and demos are happening virtually instead of in person. With technology moving so fast, you'll need to adapt your strategy to incorporate the latest advances while simultaneously showcasing what makes person-to-person sales unique. Stay abreast of new online sites and systems, and incorporate your natural creativity and skill to keep up with the digital sales world. Adapting to technological changes is important for building rapport with customers, as sales are increasingly done via online platforms (especially in the age of COVID-19).

Navigating online systems with ease will impress tech-savvy customers and give you a natural starting point for establishing a connection. Confidence with technology will also expose you to new potential customers you would never have met, relying solely on in-person sales. This is just one example of how you can create profitable connections by embracing flexibility and change.

Finally, you need to adapt your attitude and demeanor depending on your customer. Your rapport-building approach might work for the average client, but you're likely to have more than a couple tough customers who will require flexibility on your end. Some consumers view salespeople as pushy, untrustworthy, unethical, sleazy, greedy, annoying, demanding, and aggressive, while others see them as honest, helpful, trustworthy, and professional. You can't predict if you are going to be greeted by a cheerful customer or cautious cynic. Prepare yourself for either outcome. If your client already has positive associations with sales, you can approach them with an easygoing demeanor. But if they're wary of you from the start, you have to work harder and earn their respect. No matter the sale, stay flexible, and be ready to adapt.

TAKE ACTION TO MAKE THE CONNECTION

When a rep is having a hard time connecting deeply with customers, the problem always traces back to inaction. Inaction takes many forms, including call reluctance, avoidance of potential customers, and excuse-making. Sometimes all that's necessary to break the cycle of inaction is a confidence boost. Here's a helpful exercise for improving your confidence and motivating yourself to sell:

Remember a time when you faced an obstacle and overcame it. If you can't recall one, remember what it was like to learn to ride a bike. You could read about it for a long time and watch others do it, but eventually, you just had to take the leap. Maybe you skinned your knees at first, but eventually you learned to ride your bike with reckless abandon and never over-thought it again. That's like sales. The worst thing that can happen is people will say "No," hang up, or walk away. You will never get better at anything, especially selling, until you get back on that bike.

You'll never build effective rapport with customers by standing on the sidelines, waiting for them to come to you. You need to be bold and initiate the connection with a potential customer. Adapt your approach to different customers and contexts. The next section will show you how to form natural, lasting connections with clients. It's up to you to bridge the two, and take action to put yourself on the path to success.

CHAPTER SUMMARY/KEY TAKEAWAYS

In this chapter, you learned:

> **It's hard to build rapport**: Sales are the backbone of any business, but it can be difficult to build rapport when customers have changing needs and differing expectations.

> **Follow a formula**: Be inquisitive and forge genuine connections with your customers.

> **Greet**: Open with a genuine, enthusiastic greeting.

> **Relate**: Break the ice with a relatable statement or "peeling the onion" question.

> **Question**: Pose a question that will help you learn more about their business needs and improve your pitch.

> **Reflect**: Actively listen to their answers and demonstrate your interest.

> **Adapt**: In order to impress your customers, be flexible and adaptable in your approach. This means keeping up with technology, suggesting creative solutions, and being prepared for any customer.

> **Act**: Stay motivated and active every day; you won't sell without making the first move.

Now you understand how to adapt, act, and connect with customers, enabling you to build successful, engaging rapport. However, you may still feel like you aren't ready to make the sale. Afraid of failure or lacking confidence? In the next chapter, you will learn how to "Rise Up" and beat your fears.

RISE UP

Sometimes you won't feel like doing what you know you're supposed to be doing. It's easy to let fear, boredom, exhaustion, and limiting thoughts hold you back from taking action. This chapter is about avoiding those traps and growing yourself into the kind of person who executes, not the type who makes excuses. You'll learn to take action even when you don't feel like it.

If fear keeps you from rising up, I'll show you how to beat it down into submission in this chapter. You'll then learn the nine traits that will enable you to conquer each day instead of letting the day overwhelm you. Finally, you'll build a toolkit to help you through your worst days.

FIGHT YOUR FEAR

If you're not careful, fear can control your life and squander your potential. Many mediocre sellers end up full of regret due to chances not taken and dreams not chased. Sales isn't a career for the timid. If you don't learn how to dominate your fears and rise up, you risk leading a life towards regret.

Most people, myself included, don't like to admit the extent to which fear rules our lives. Instead, we often generate a litany of excuses for why something didn't work out. Recall a time you had a wild idea and were excited to share it with friends and family, only to have them respond, "That's crazy!" or "That will never work." They likely wanted to protect you from harm or disappointment, but they also might have inadvertently been holding you back from a fantastic achievement. After all, the world was built on crazy ideas. The Thomas Edisons and Steve Jobs of the world are the ones who said, "I'm not going to be sidelined by my fear or people's doubts. I'm willing to take a leap of faith and try something great." Stop making excuses and buying into others' doubts. Don't discount your dreams. Get up and go make them happen.

Two former employees at Microsoft, Whit Alexander and Richard Tait ignored the feedback of many to pursue their own "crazy-ass idea:" leaving their jobs to create a board game. Both had successful careers that were rewarding and stable inside Microsoft. Neither had any experience with designing and marketing a board game. But they had conviction and an entrepreneurial spirit and seized a unique opportunity to sell their game in a non-traditional way by offering it for sale inside Starbucks. Since they were living and working in the Seattle area where Starbucks was founded, getting connected with the right people to pitch their idea was a matter of leveraging their network. Richard had climbed Mt. Kilimanjaro with someone who paved the way for him to speak with Starbucks' CEO, Howard Schultz. The result was a runaway hit that became "Game of the Year" in 2001.[7] In a 2003 interview with Fast Company, Tait's advice to would-be entrepreneurs was a message on how to beat fear. "Orville Wright did not have a pilot's license: don't ever be afraid to bend, or even break the rules.".[8] Fear is our body's warning

---

[7]   "Inside the Smartest Little Company in America," Inc.com, last modified January 1, 2002, https://www.inc.com/magazine/20020101/23798.html.

[8]   Fast C. Staff, "Richard Tait – Fast 50 2003," Fast Company, last modified December 4, 2013, https://www.

signal, and its job is to protect us from adverse outcomes. One of the most potent forces contributing to fear is social comparison, which involves focusing on the expectations of other people. A recent study in neuroscience found people experienced reduced feelings of regret and took fewer risks when a social comparison was favorable (i.e. when they believed others would approve their planned actions).[9] We like to take steps others support, and deviating from the norm is scary. But by living our lives to make others happy and limiting our ambitions, we run the risk of carrying regret into the future. In a recent study, people who experienced a greater sense of regret were more likely to take dangerous risks in the future to compensate.[10] Are you placing too much value on what others think? An essential part of rising up is resisting the fear associated with social comparison. Lori Grenier of TV's "Shark Tank" offers up this wise advice: "Don't let people who were afraid to pursue their dreams try to talk you out of pursuing yours".[11] It's been proven that people with high self-esteem tend to ignore what others think and don't let others' expectations influence their actions.[12] So, to conquer fear, you've got to learn to temper the input of others and follow your intuition.

Nearly everyone can think of something they've always wanted to do but have avoided because they fear a negative response from others. For me, I always wanted to become a pilot. I wrote a letter to Captain Gordon, the radio broadcaster who reported on the traffic in Syracuse, NY. He responded and invited my mother and I for my

---

fastcompany.com/1539035/richard-tait-fast-50-2003.

9   Zhiyuan Liu et al., "Social comparison modulates the neural responses to regret and subsequent risk-taking behavior," *Social Cognitive and Affective Neuroscience* 13, no. 10 (2018): xx, doi:10.1093/scan/nsy066.

10   Eyal Winter, Ph.D., "The Fear of Regret and Its Consequences," *Psychology Today*, last modified February 14, 2019, https://www.psychologytoday.com/us/blog/feeling-smart/201902/the-fear-regret-and-its-consequences.

11   Greiner, L. (2019, July 22). lorigreinershark. Retrieved from Instagram: 2019

12   Anthony D. Hermann, Geoffrey J. Leonardelli, and Robert M. Arkin, "Self-Doubt and Self-Esteem: A Threat from within," *Personality and Social Psychology Bulletin* 28, no. 3 (2002): xx, doi:10.1177/0146167202286010.

first airplane flight. It led me to pursue a career in the US Air Force. I applied to Undergraduate Pilot Training and took an aptitude test. When I received my results, I was told, "Your results mean that *you will never* be a pilot." I believed this and allowed it to hold me back for over a decade. Finally, I realized this one test and opinion didn't define me; my ambition and my passion were my own to chase. I started training again and eventually received a 98 on my pilot test and have been flying high ever since.

Where would our world be if people throughout history didn't rise up and get past their fears? One of my favorite examples is the story of Colonel Harland Sanders, the founder of Kentucky Fried Chicken. After his successful restaurant suffered from a decrease in traffic, Sanders took a bold approach: he sold his business, lived in his car, and traveled the country selling his recipe to prospective franchisees.[13] At age 74, he finally succeeded. Now you can find a KFC in every major city on the planet, all because Col. Sanders knew in his gut that he was destined for more.

Reflect on some of the people who made the world better by bravely overcoming their fears. Think about Abraham Lincoln. With the country in chaos from the Civil War, he wrote and delivered The Gettysburg Address against his advisors' advice, advocating that freedom would unify the country.[14] Walt Disney chased his dream despite failure and criticism.[15] Thomas Edison continued forward despite a series of setbacks and failures. He famously declared, "I have not failed 10,000 times. I have not failed once. I have succeeded

13   "The Tragic, Real-life Story of Colonel Sanders," Mashed.com, last modified October 22, 2019, https://www.mashed.com/131055/the-tragic-real-life-story-of-colonel-sanders/.

14   "The Gettysburg Address by Abraham Lincoln," Abraham Lincoln Online Your Source for Lincoln News and Information, accessed November 8, 2020, https://www.abrahamlincolnonline.org/lincoln/speeches/gettysburg.htm.

15   Steven Watts, The Magic Kingdom: Walt Disney and the American Way of Life (Columbia: University of Missouri Press, 2013)

in proving that those 10,000 ways will not work. When I have eliminated the ways that will not work, I will find a way to work".[16]

Many people avoid a rewarding sales career out of fear. They fear public speaking, defending their ideas, asking others for commitment, rejection, and failure. We all fear these things. But to be truly successful in sales, you need to learn to overcome these fears. Really, the only thing you need to *be afraid of is fear itself.* Whenever you recognize fear's telltale signs — sweating, increased breathing, heart rate, butterflies — take those indicators and turn them into action. Internalize the fact that people have survived fear for thousands of years. Stand up to your fear monster and march forward with the courage and conviction that you're going to be alright. You must practice living with and overcoming fear.

Prepare for sales meetings that scare you. Two of my mentors, Gene and Art, taught me the 7 "P" Principle: Proper Prior Planning Prevents Piss Poor Performance. Follow these 7 "P"s to make preparation a habit. Practice and repetition will help you overcome your fears. Stand in front of fictional crowds to practice before a big speech or presentation, and you'll find yourself overcoming stage fright.

Overcoming your fears is the first step on your journey to becoming a person of action. You're the main character in your story, it's time to start acting like it. Mediocre salespeople know what to do but make excuses for not following through. To be a superstar seller, you have to take action when others give up. The next section will teach you the essential qualities you need to take control of your career and your future. Develop these traits, and you'll be ready to rise up every day.

16   Nathan Furr, "How Failure Taught Edison to Repeatedly Innovate," Forbes, last modified August 9, 2011, https://www.forbes.com/sites/nathanfurr/2011/06/09/how-failure-taught-edison-to-repeatedly-innovate/#4bfb3b8465e9.

9 SUPERSTAR TRAITS TO RISE UP

Attitude

Your attitude determines your altitude. A Native American proverb calls us to make the most of every day because "when the sun sets, it takes a part of your life with it." You must make the most of each day, and that starts with a positive attitude. Are you going to be someone who lifts the spirits of yourself and others? Or are you going to get your coffee and grumble through the day complaining? The choice is entirely yours, but remember that every breath exhaled is gone forever. Attitude is the octane in your tank to get you going and is entirely under your control.

My dad used to tell me he hated the word "can't." When I struggled with my Spanish classes, he would say, "Tell yourself Spanish is hard, but if you apply yourself, seek out help from teachers, and practice, you will be able to learn it." It was a handy trick for improving my attitude.

Here are a few ideas on building a better attitude:

> Surround yourself with people you want to emulate.

> Feed yourself positivity. What you read and listen to should uplift and inspire you, not bring you down.

> Watch your self-talk. Are you telling yourself you *can't* do something? Be careful what you tell yourself. You might believe it.

> Commit to having a positive day from the start. Wake up with gratitude and determination, and carry those mindsets throughout your day.

Empathy

Believe it or not, empathy is an important part of your job. You need to develop a client-centric approach to everything you do. If you are creating a sales proposal, think about reading it from the receiver's standpoint. One of my first sales managers, Jessica, shared with me that people don't care how much you know until they know how much you care. People buy from people who care about them. Think about companies and sales professionals whom you buy from repeatedly. It's probably not only because of their prices or products, but because they care to make the buying experience more about you than themselves.

Early in my sales career, I presented a proposal for a sales automation solution, and my customer had a heart attack. People often say jokingly that their customers react that way to great deals, but this customer had a real medical emergency right in the middle of my sales pitch. Of course, we started CPR and got him prompt medical attention. Since he had traveled out of his country for this meeting, we also visited him in the hospital and brought him flowers to make him feel comfortable. This was a unique situation, but showing genuine empathy for your customers is an important part of making them feel comfortable with you.

Empathy also played an essential role in a real estate investment of mine. I arrived for a showing at a house I was interested in and was disappointed to see junk and newspapers piling up on the porch. It looked like no one lived there, but eventually, the owner answered the door. Jim slowly maneuvered a walker as he greeted me with a big smile on his face, but his legs were swollen and discolored. He asked if I could help pick up the newspapers on his porch. I could see from the look on his face that he was struggling. Jim shared that an accident in his woodshop had nearly killed him. A rusted piece of metal flew into his leg, and he endured months of treatment for a blood infection. After being put out of work, his wife of 26 years left him. Jim showed me his house and his woodshop, which were immaculate. I could tell this was a proud and caring person whose misfortune had turned his life upside down.

Before I left, I picked up all the newspapers on his front porch, swept it clean, and helped him make a phone call to his daughter. I had planned on negotiating a sale with Jim, but instead, I just listened and tried to help him with his needs. When I left Jim that day, I didn't "close" him. I told him to call me if he needed anything and that I would pray for him. I no longer thought of Jim's house as a "prospective investment;" I cared about his well-being. After three weeks, Jim asked me to buy his place from him, and I did. I also helped him move to his daughter's house and cried after seeing how happy he was as he got the help he needed. A prospective investment turned into a genuine human connection, and the transaction was so much more rewarding.

Empathy is something to practice every day. People are fighting their own battles, and a little compassion goes a long way. Just remember every sales interaction involves a living, breathing human being with feelings, dreams, and aspirations. You can express empathy in an email, it doesn't have to be a big deal. The only requirement is a willingness to put yourself in another person's shoes. Being empathetic means suspending judgment and meeting people where they are. The Cheyenne people admonished each other not to judge others until you've walked two moons in their moccasins. When you learn to live your life with more empathy, rising up to the challenges you face will become more meaningful.

Resiliency

Life is full of setbacks; if you're going to rise to the challenges of sales, you need to be able to bounce back quickly. When sales don't go well, the best approach is to seek feedback, correct what you can, and try again. One of my managers used to say, "Let's not get more than 20 steps outside the main entrance before we share feedback of what worked and what didn't." I call this the 20 Steps Rule, and I still follow it today. Consistently looking for what worked and what didn't will make you more comfortable with small failures and will help create a culture of continuous improvement. This type of self-reflection will make you more resilient.

Authenticity

Finding and embodying your authentic self will imbue you with the confidence to rise up. Authenticity is important in sales because it forces you to be more vulnerable, which helps you to connect with your customer. But being authentic is hard in today's world. We are constantly bombarded with images and suggestions of how we should look, dress, and act. To become more authentic, you have to let go of a lot of inner junk that doesn't matter and work on developing the best version of yourself.

Own up to the fact that we are all imperfect people living in an imperfect world. To be authentic means humbly admitting that the invisible sign you wear will always say "under construction." While you may have mastery in various areas, there is still room for improvement.

Accountability and mentorship will also help you be more authentic. Finding partners who are invested in helping you grow and hold you accountable for your shortcomings is a recipe for meaningful growth. Surround yourself with the type of people who will respectfully call you out on your BS and blindspots. It can be challenging to share honest, negative feedback with the people we care about, but it is so important. Establish a precedent of honesty and accountability with the people around you. Let them know you value their input and won't hold any vendettas against them if they speak the truth.

It's also important to be authentic with yourself. Do you find yourself saying, "I'm going to work out, I'm going to eat better, I'm not going to gossip," but then do those exact things? When you become more honest with yourself, you will become more open with those around you as a result, and you'll be on your way to living your life with more authenticity.

Passion

Passion is about tapping into what drives you and capitalizing on the emotion it stirs to inspire you to rise up. Bestselling author Simon Sinek said, "Working hard for something we don't care about is called stress. Working hard for something we love is called passion".[17] Research has defined passion as "an individual's emotional and per-sistent state of desire based on cognitive and affective work appraisals, which results in consistent work intentions and behaviors."[18]

When you are pouring your efforts into something you love, passion shows. The work seems effortless. It gets you up in the morning and is the reason you endure late nights and long hours. Passion grows internally and manifests outwardly. Why are you passionate about sales? Identify the driving force and use it to motivate yourself.

17   "Twitter," Welcome to Twitter, accessed November 8, 2020, https://twitter.com/simonsinek/status/174469085726375936.

18   Pamela L. Perrewé et al., "Developing a passion for work passion: Future directions on an emerging construct," *Journal of Organizational Behavior* 35, no. 1 (2013): 145-150, doi:10.1002/job.1902.

Confidence

Confidence is essential when it's time for you to rise up. It's a delicate balance, though; being too confident can make you reckless, which can be as detrimental as timidity. I remember using a profiling scale for new hires with ego on one side and intellect on the other. Anyone who strayed too far towards one of the extremes was an undesirable candidate. Too much confidence and your ego will drive your actions; not enough, and you'll struggle to relate to others. The right balance of confidence will allow you to excel in any situation and rise up in the face of challenges.

Commitment

If you're going to rise to face the challenges in your way, you need to commit yourself fully. Commitment starts with small promises, but if people trust you to stick to your word about the little things, you'll soon be trusted to tackle bigger things. Developing your commitment means showing up for the mission every day and doing what you said you would even when no one is looking. Become the type of person who can be counted on.

In business, a lack of commitment can cripple a sales team and destroy morale. I once worked for a company where everyone on the team ruthlessly competed against each other, even to the point of stealing leads. On my first day, the office manager told me to make sure I locked my desk at the end of the day. When I asked whether there was a problem with crime in the building, she answered that I shouldn't give anyone an advantage. People stole leads and tips from each other whenever they could. It was a cut-throat environment, and you couldn't count on anyone. I stayed with them for a month, then decided I wanted to work somewhere coworkers were

BILLION DOLLAR SALES SECRETS

committed to the team, not only to themselves. Find an environment that fosters a sense of communal commitment, and you'll be inspired to rise up every day.

Focus

Rich, successful people maintain a high degree of focus, allowing them to rise to any challenge that comes their way. Staying focused helps you devote 100% of your attention to your goals and will enable you to work smarter and more efficiently. Focused people live by their calendars and keep their appointments; this type of goal-directed behavior makes them successful. While writing this book, I often listened to brain.fm, a radio station designed to improve concentration.

The team at brain.fm has researched how auditory stimulation enhances focus. It's fascinating, and I noticed I could write considerably more words when I tuned in. Focus is the gas in your tank. It fuels achievement and allows you to tune out the noise.

Discipline

Finally, discipline is the last trait that will help you rise up. Discipline is the art of doing what is necessary, even when you have no drive left. It's the practice of sticking to your habits and goals, even when no one is looking. It's about putting in the work instead of taking the easy way out. There will be days when you have to get your butt up out of bed and grind to reach your goals. You'll have to make friends with discipline if you want to get good at selling.

CONQUERING DOUBT AND BAD DAYS

Even with these superstar traits, you're going to have good days and bad days. You need to expect both to overcome and rise up. Your bad days are the ones when you feel so exhausted you think about calling it quits or when you let a negative mindset infect your work. Rising up means facing these days with courage. You'll have numerous setbacks, especially if you're trying something no one has done before. The people around you might say you are wasting your time or following a fool's dream. It's easy to doubt yourself when everyone else already does. Here are some tools for conquering these bad days:

➤ Write down annual goals, create plans to achieve them, track your progress, and check in monthly.

➤ Develop visual representations of your dreams. This could take the form of a "dream board," inspirational screensaver, or motivating photo taped to your bathroom mirror.

➤ Listen to songs that cheer you up on your bad days.

➤ Create an invigorating starting ritual. When your alarm clock rings and your eyes first open, what is your automatic reaction? What is your first thought? Try writing a word on an index card and attaching it to your alarm clock to help you focus before your feet hit the floor. Words like fearless, bravery, dream, humble, and thankful will encourage you to start your day with mindfulness and intention.

➤ Save the awards, letters of commendation, and congratulatory notes you've received over the years. Put them in a box and read them on the bad days or when you doubt yourself.

CHAPTER SUMMARY/KEY TAKEAWAYS

In this chapter, you learned:

> **Life is full of setbacks and excuses**: You'll always have a reason to give up. Rising up means pushing forward even when all you want to do is call it quits.

> **Master your fears**: Don't let your fears control you. They'll only hold you back. Fear itself is the only thing to be scared of.

> **9 traits to rise up**: Develop these traits to learn how to rise up:

  → **Attitude**: Attitude determines altitude. You're in control of your mindset, so make it a good one.

  → **Empathy**: Empathy goes a long way in sales. Make sure you put yourself in your customer's shoes and show them you care.

  → **Resiliency**: You won't go through life without getting knocked down a bit, and sales is no different. All that matters is getting back up each time.

  → **Authenticity**: Be authentic to those around you *and* to yourself. Your clients will appreciate your transparency.

  → **Passion**: Don't forget what motivates you. You'll have to rely on your passion when you're exhausted, overworked, and ready to quit.

  → **Confidence**: People respond positively to confidence. Keep your ego in check and project calm confidence to stay at the top of your game.

  → **Commitment**: You have to be all in. Do the little things well, and the big things will follow.

  → **Focus**: Don't let distractions keep you from working

towards your dreams. Concentrate your energy and get ready to rise.

→ **Discipline**: Rising up means keeping your head down and grinding, even on the days you'd rather not.

➤ **Conquer your bad days**: You'll have doubts and difficult days. Rely on motivational tools to get through them.

Now that you know how to conquer your fears, develop superstar traits, and beat the bad days, you're ready to rise up and meet the challenges facing you. Next, you'll learn how to take this energy and channel it into developing a plan for success.

IT TAKES A PLAN

Planning well is easier said than done. You want to shoot high, but avoid creating a plan so fantastical that executing it is unrealistic. Your plan has to be detailed; you need to spend the time breaking it down into subparts. In this chapter, you will learn how to craft strategies for success. First, I'll explain why it's essential to dream big. You'll then learn the relationship between plans, processes, and progress, the key types of plans you need to create, and my unique process for accomplishing your plans. Finally, I'll show you how to evaluate your progress.

START WITH A DREAM

If you're going to plan for success, you need a dream to chase. In this section, I'll teach you how to cultivate bold dreams instead of accepting mediocrity. Stop for a second and reflect on what your dreams are. If you're not tracking your dreams, you're likely an actor in someone else's dream. You just don't recognize it yet.

I've dared to dream big in my career, and it's paid off time and again. Every year when I look at my sales quotas I ask myself "What will it take to reach 300% of that number?" Meeting 100% of my quota means I am simply doing my job. Meeting 300% means I am exceptional. One year, not only did I reach 472% of my quota, but I did it in half the time. I dreamed a bigger dream for myself and succeeded beyond my wildest imagination.

When salespeople strive to achieve only what's expected, they set the bar too low for themselves. I think some of this is the way we were brought up in school. Earning 100% on a report or paper was celebrated, but what about going above and beyond? As adults, we've grown to believe that achieving someone else's goal for us is the same as reaching our own. You need to detach yourself from others' dreams and come up with bigger and better goals for yourself. Internalize the practice of dreaming big; only then can you create your plan for success.

It's more important than ever to dream big today. COVID-19 has accelerated innovation at dramatic rates. As the situation changes daily, smart businesses that aren't afraid to dream up new solutions continue to succeed. Companies that once manufactured cheerleading uniforms have retooled to make PPE for health workers. Food production companies that once catered to restaurants shifted their model to the consumer segment. Plastic manufacturers are creating face shields and dividers for grocery stores and casinos. Necessity is the mother of invention, and even during tough times – it pays to dream.

You shortchange yourself in life by not dreaming big. You owe it to yourself to think about what is possible. You may not believe it yet, but setting your bar higher works. Reflect on the following questions: Why am I not dreaming bigger? What can I achieve if I set my sights higher? Somebody's dreams have to come true; why not mine?

PLAN, PROCESS, PROGRESS

Now that you're dreaming bigger, you're ready to create your path to success. Selling can be complicated, and the best way to deal with complexity is to prepare. Your preparation includes an ironclad plan, a detailed process for executing your plan, and a progress assessment. I can trace every failed sale back to a mistake in the execution of my plan. Planning and discipline will allow you to overcome obstacles as you encounter them.

Before we go into detail, let's start with some basic definitions of your tools:

> **The plan**: The plan is your recipe for success. It includes all the things you need to do and when. You need sales plans for every meeting you have with customers, plans for taking advantage of every opportunity, and plans for maintaining important business relationships. You wouldn't take a road trip to the Alaskan wilderness without a plan. Why would you "wing it" when it comes to selling? Your plan provides direction and a guide for the sale. This chapter will give you detailed instructions for planning.

> **The process**: These are the steps that take your sale from inception to close. Think of the process as a detailed map. You know where you're starting from, where you want to finish, and the major steps along the way. Having a process allows you to go back and analyze where things went wrong after you lose a sale. In this chapter you will learn more about the sales funnel, the sales ladder, and how to develop your own sales process.

> **Progress assessment**: Finally, you must assess what you've

done. Tony Horton, the creator of P90X, says, "How do you know what to do if you don't know what you've done?" Your plans and processes guide your sale, but you need to analyze your progress along the way. Customer relationship management (CRM) tools offer many great reports and metrics to help you with this task. Consistently analyzing progress allows you to identify gaps in competency, weaknesses, and areas for improvement. Your plan and process are nothing if you don't regularly reflect on your progress.

PLAN

When you don't have a plan, you risk losing control of a sale. I recently went to the Tesla store, genuinely curious about their cars. The sales professional was excellent and communicated the value of owning a Tesla. He took control of the sale by saying to me, "We should get you an appointment to come drive one of these." I thought it was a good idea too, and agreed. Then he asked for my name, phone number, and email and said, "I'm going to email you to set up a time, ok?" He had control of the sale and led me through the process of saying yes. He could have easily said, "Hey, it was nice showing you these cars. Have a great day!" Instead, he took control and earned my business.

In sales, you rely on plans to identify the desired outcome and your path forward. There are many different types of plans, and this section will give you a quick overview of a few before going into depth about how to plan your sales calls and opportunities. Some basic plans to be familiar with include:

➤ **Business plan**: The broadest type of plan, business plans, involve time-bound goals to ensure your business's success.

They are both internally and externally facing, considering company and customer goals. A time-tested method utilized in by many is SWOT analysis: strengths, weaknesses, opportunities, and threats.

> **Territory plan**: These plans are more specialized to the territory you will be selling in, and are important to create if you're entering a new market or industry.

> **Account plan**: Functioning on a smaller scale, these plans focus on creating a path forward for an individual customer. They involve detailed analysis of customer needs and values, and allow you to plan your approach for a specific account.

Now let's get into the two plans that will be most important in your career: Sales Call Plans and Opportunity Plans.

Sales Call Planning

You're going out on a sales call. How do you prepare? Never wing it! You must do some pre-call planning in order to have something to guide your meeting and a way to evaluate if it was a success or not. Let's break down the Sales Call Plan now, so you will know how to create one effectively. These are the critical elements for a good Sales Call Plan:

1. **Purpose**: What do you want to accomplish and why?

2. **Desired Outcome**: Know what success looks like. Think of the best possible outcome in unambiguous terms. Let's say you're a realtor meeting with a customer. Your best possible outcome might be to understand all the details of the seller's situation and property so that you can prepare a

listing agreement. Beyond the desired outcome, know your minimum acceptable outcome. If your meeting produces a result in between those benchmarks, then it is a success.

3. **Benefit**: What specific benefits will the customer realize as a result of their time with you? Think about what you bring to the table.

4. **Attendees**: Who will be in the meeting, what are their roles, and what do you know about them? Have you looked at their social media accounts to see if you have any common ground or interests? Try to put yourself in their shoes – what would you expect from a meeting with you?

5. **Topics**: What issues have you agreed to discuss? How do they support your mutually defined objectives? Be prepared for the small talk and introductions at the start of the meeting by coming prepared with questions about common interests.

6. **Time**: When is the meeting, and how long will it be? If you schedule an appointment for an hour, be there at least 15-20 minutes before the meeting. Don't arrive at the last minute and expect to jump right in. Think about the time required to travel to the location and set up; it's not a bad idea to pad the time a bit if you get lost or hit traffic. And if you achieve your objectives early, close the meeting and give people their time back. There is no reason to keep a discussion going for an hour if you accomplished your goal in 30 minutes.

7. **Location**: Where will this take place, in person or virtual? What do you know about the setting? Location is critical. One of the worst meetings I had was during my time in

real estate. I went to evaluate a property and when I arrived the place looked a little scary. Inside, I found out it was a meth house. A woman was injecting drugs into her arm, the place was trashed, and guns were everywhere. Knowing your location matters, and this knowledge may even save your life. On a more practical note, considerations like WiFi, ADA accessible facilities, and security are important to research in advance.

8. **Impact & Follow Up**: What will you do to leave an impact? Do you have anything to share to help your customer remember you long after you left? Any leave-behinds, presentation samples, follow-ups? Think about what you want the customer to do once you leave, and make an impression that will inspire this action. Then make sure to follow up later!

Your plan is unique to your sale, and will depend on your industry, your business, your client, and much more. Plans aren't "one size fits all," and you need to ask yourself lots of questions and do your research before laying down your plan. Lucky for you, I've created a few online templates to help you think through your sales call planning. Just go to www.billiondollarsalessecrets.com, create a login, and go to the free downloads section. Next, you'll learn about another critical type of plan to help you improve your strategy.

Opportunity Planning

A sales opportunity is a potential alignment of value between your business offering and a customer. Opportunity planning will allow you to identify and assess these prospects. Opportunity plans involve sales criteria that refine your opportunity focus. Sales criteria indicate the elements needed for a potential opportunity to be worthy of your time and energy. Looking at the criteria collectively allows you to plan your reaction to the opportunity. Standard criteria are Need, Urgency, Approval, Authority, Vision, and Action. Let's look at how these determine if you have a viable prospect:

1. **Need**: What condition can you help fulfill? If your customer doesn't have a need, you likely don't have a sales opportunity. However, sometimes the customer's needs are unknown, especially if you sell a solution that has never been sold before. You may have to dig deeper to determine if your customer has a latent need. There are generally two types of needs, expressed or latent. Expressed needs are easy to identify and are addressed by the current market, while latent needs are not being served. Most customers have not been challenged enough to recognize their latent needs.

2. **Urgency**: When does the customer need this solution? More importantly, why do they need it in this specific timeframe? What is driving their timing for this product or solution? To understand urgency, it helps to understand the Eisenhower Principle. In 1954, Eisenhower declared, "What is important is seldom urgent, and what is urgent is seldom important," thus establishing the Eisenhower Principle. There are four quadrants of time management: Important and Urgent, Important and Not Urgent, Not Important and Urgent, Not Important and Not Urgent. People buy for many reasons, but typically they never buy unless there is some form of urgency. This is why it's important to know the timeframe and urgency of your customer's needs. In March and April 2020, I witnessed firsthand the power of urgency

as companies dealt with the impact of COVID-19. Everything had a heightened urgency, and I saw more companies transforming to digital business in sixty days than I had my entire career. People and companies will prioritize time and resources based on urgency. So, find out where your product fits in.

3. **Approval**: Understanding the approval process is critical in planning for the likelihood of a successful sales opportunity. Don't assume your first contact is the decision maker. Identify the decision makers. Understand the entire approval *process* and all of the people who are part of it. Once you understand how decisions are made, you'll know if the prospect is a good fit.

4. **Authority**: Now that you understand the process, you need to understand the players. Ultimately, someone has the authority to make your sale happen. Who is it? Authority often isn't based on titles; someone may have an impressive title but lack influence. Authority is complex, and you may have to work hard to identify who has it.

5. **Vision**: Your prospective customer has to envision themselves as a buyer and perceive enough value to commit. Help them visualize a successful close to the sale and imagine the benefits they'll reap. Describing in detail the positive outcomes will help create that vision for them.

6. **Action**: Is your customer or prospective customer going to take action to explore the possibility of doing business with you further? If so, you've identified a strong potential sale. When the other party has a willingness to take action, it makes your job that much easier.

The goal of your opportunity plan is to evaluate your opportunity critically and decide how to plan for successful closure. Your opportunity plan is a strategic analysis that serves as your opportunity strategy document, and it's essential to your success.

Now that you understand sales call and opportunity planning, make sure to create an action plan outlining the entire series of steps needed to get to your goal. I generally like to share this with customers and co-develop it. Remember, selling is something you do *with* customers, not to them. Why not bring the process out in the open and understand how their business functions? Then build a robust action plan with dates and accountabilities for each step of the way. The customer appreciates the knowledge of what will happen next and how they can plan for it. When you spell this out and discuss the actions that need to occur, who is accountable and set realistic timelines, you have a path to a successful sale. Now that you know how to plan, the next section will show you what you need to execute your plan: a process.

PROCESS

With a plan in place, you'll need a process to follow that plan.

The Sales Ladder System™

After years of trial and error in sales, I created this system, and you can use my discovery to excel. The sales process requires you to take strategic steps to align your value with your customer. To illustrate this, imagine a ladder representing value alignment between you and your customer: on one side of the ladder is the customer, and on the other is the seller. You start the sales process together on the ground, and you must climb rung by rung to the top to reach the sale. Each rung represents shared value creation between you and the customer, and you must build them together. Your goal is to establish successful value connections (the rungs) to build to the sale (the top).

If your ladder rungs become uneven, symbolic of you and your customer being misaligned, your sale is in danger. Balance each rung of value as you progress upward toward your goal. You also must climb quickly because beneath you is time, acting as fire and burning up past value. Don't hesitate too long, or else the ladder will collapse.

The sales ladder relies on successful value alignment, so let's look at some different elements of value alignment:

> **Time**: Understand the time frame of your sale. Is this a deal that is good for a day, a week, a month, or sometime in the next year? Make sure you and the customer are clear and in agreement about the deal's timing. It serves as one of the most important rungs on your ladder.

> **Competition**: It pays to know your competition, and there is always a competitive threat to your sale. Your job is to be Sherlock Holmes. Identify competitive pressures and deduce how they impact your value alignment. You may think you know your competitors by heart, but some are less obvious, such as the inaction competitor. After all your selling, the customer may choose not to act. Understanding your competition is rooted in how well your value aligns with your customer's. Do you know how your competition aligns?

> **Influence**: In opportunity planning, we looked at authority. However, it also pays to understand who the influencers are. These are all the people who have a stake or may influence the sale. Understand what is driving them toward a successful

outcome. Knowing the influencers of the sale and charting them out in your opportunity plan gives you clarity and will allow you to improve your value alignment with your customer.

As you evaluate the areas where you hope to build value, assess whether any of these factors need to be strengthened. You might look at pricing, for instance, as one of the rungs on the ladder. When you evaluate pricing from your side, it may be okay. But if the customer thinks it's too high, they can shop around for alternatives. The reality from their perspective may be that this rung of your ladder is uneven and needs to be shored up. What could you do to level this value? Maybe you could give a discount or offer to help market the solution. Analyze which rungs are unsteady, and look for opportunities to solidify those value alignments.

Look at your ladder: you know the dates, the steps, the rungs of value to build on, and what alignment looks like with your customer. Use the system to communicate where you are in the process and where you are going. A technique known as "signposting" makes it easier for your prospective customers to know where they are on the journey with you and how to align your values better. The Sales Ladder System™ is a simple way to visually check whether you align with your customer and see what is needed to get into alignment. We have sample plans for you to review at www.billiondollarsalessecrets.com.

The Sales Funnel

A popular process is the sales funnel. Many successful businesses use the funnel to represent the sales process visually. The funnel is wide at the top and narrows into a pipeline at the bottom. At the top of the funnel, usually, outside, you have the target marketplace of prospective customers and new opportunities. Once you've established criteria for an opportunity, customers enter into the funnel. The funnel is larger at the top to accommodate many potential customers at first. But as your potential customers move through the sales process, they will either become more mutually aligned to your values and goals, or they will drop out of the funnel. Those who reach the bottom are well aligned with your values, and the criteria are right to complete the sale. The sales funnel is a basic visual to understand how opportunities flow through your process. To be effective, though, you need to overlay your specific process onto the funnel.

To create your sales process, bring your team together to understand and document your typical sale. Sales process creation usually involves all departments to ensure you have a correct and comprehensive depiction of the process. Putting your process into steps makes it easier to overlay your strategy into a sales automation system or a customer relationship management (CRM) system. In the graphic below of a sales funnel, I've also overlaid a generic sales process. Whether you visualize your process with a ladder or a funnel, make sure to follow the steps to your customer to ensure mutual value alignment and set yourself up for success.

GENERIC SALES FUNNEL

DISCOVERY - QUALIFY

DEVELOP SOLUTION OR REQUIREMENTS

PROPOSAL OR PROTOTYPE

EVALUATION

NEGOTIATE - CLOSE

PROGRESS

You've dreamed big, planned your sale, and are executing the process. Now you need a way to track and evaluate your progress. Progress assessments let you know if you're on track for success or if you've stalled and need to rethink your approach. There are several ways to evaluate your progress, and in this section, you'll learn about key performance indicators (KPIs) and my 20 Step Sales Call Review.

According to the Balanced Scorecard Institute, good KPIs are evidence of progress toward your goal.[19] They measure what's needed to inform decision making and show trends over time. KPIs involve leading and lagging indicators: leading indicators are used to refer to performance metrics, and lagging indicators measure result metrics. You need to analyze your KPIs to be an effective seller. It's impossible to gauge and measure progress without looking at what's working and what's not working. For instance, you might want to understand your conversion rate, or how many calls, marketing materials, or engagements it takes before you convert to your desired action (a sale, a callback, or a click on a website). The simple formula is:

**(# of desired outcomes achieved / # of attempts) x 100
= conversion rate %**

Other metrics to measure include value of sales, time spent in each stage of the process, and total sales stuck in the cycle for greater than 90 days. Most CEOs analyze profits and growth as their KPIs, and you'll want to consider tracking these as well as sales profitability, sales revenue growth, and customer engagement. It's helpful to get data about your progress. Most CRM solutions come with built-in

---

19 "Key Performance Indicators (KPIs)," Strategy Management Group, last modified May 28, 2020, https://strategymanage.com/solutions/kpi-solution/?__hstc=51463094.26b2f76dfa7c5d2ff2bd2ffcd49bb84c.1604865857055.1604

metrics to evaluate performance, and a data-centric approach will enable you to easily mark progress and stay on a continuous journey of improvement.

Another way I like to evaluate progress is with my 20 Step Sales Call Review. After an in-person sales call, I take 20 steps outside the door and then review with my team how the call went. Did we achieve our objectives for the meeting? Did we land between our minimum and best possible outcome? What investments did we make up to that point, and was it worth it? If we don't see the results you wanted, we analyze the metrics to determine the next best step. The information and feedback from regular progress assessments help manage time and energy and keep teams on track with their goals.

CHAPTER SUMMARY/KEY TAKEAWAYS

In this chapter, you learned:

> **Planning is essential but difficult**: You can't "wing it" in sales. Coming up with a comprehensive plan and process for your sale is challenging, time-consuming, and necessary.

> **Dream first**: Before you start planning, push yourself to dream big. Aim for 300% of what people expect of you and never settle for less.

> **Plan**: Selling involves plans of all types and sizes.

>> **Sales Call Planning**: Create a detailed plan for your sales calls, including Purpose, Desired Outcome, Benefit, Attendees, Topics, Time, Location, Impact, and Follow Up.

>> **Opportunity Planning**: Plan your response to prospective opportunities by utilizing the following criteria: Need, Urgency, Approval, Authority, Vision, and Action.

> **Process**: You have a plan. Now you need to commit to a detailed process for executing it and securing the sale.

>> **The Sales Ladder System™**: Establish successful value alignments with your customer to create the rungs of your ladder and climb together to the sale at the top.

>> **The Sales Funnel**: Overlay your specific process on top of the sales funnel and allow it to help you move potential customers through the pipeline.

> **Progress**: Analyze your progress consistently along the way, utilizing data, metrics, KPIs, and the 20 Step Sales Call Review.

Now that you know how to plan for your sale, it's time to learn about the most unpredictable factor in selling: People. People make selling both exciting and challenging, and in the next chapter I will share some secrets about how to deal with all the characters you will meet.

HIGH-QUALITY CONNECTIONS

You can have perfectly laid plans, flawless processes, and consistent progress assessments and still not make the sale. Why? Because people are unpredictable. Sales is inherently a people-focused business, so you need to get used to the surprises, challenges, and possibilities that come with humanity. Every sales interaction will be unique, even if you know the customer well. Just as you have your own biases and baggage, your customers carry beliefs and predispositions you'll never be able to fully predict. We are all in a constant state of change, so you can never know what to expect when you meet someone. As Forrest Gump said, "Life is like a box of chocolates, you never know what you're going to get."[20] The same is true of people.

When you conduct post-mortem reviews of unsuccessful sales, you'll likely find the root of the problem traces back to people. You can have excellent plans and products, but if your customer suddenly decides they don't need what you're selling, there's not much you can do. Perhaps you invested your time with the wrong person, and failed

---

20   *Forrest Gump*. Paramount Pictures; 1994.

to see who had the influence to approve your sale. Or maybe your potential customer simply had a bad day. A well-intentioned salesperson once called me on the day my mother died. Everything up to that point in the sale had been positive, and I'm sure the salesperson forecast a high likelihood that we would close. In a moment, people's lives can change drastically, so you need to be cognizant of where your customer is at.

You need to love meeting new people to succeed in sales. This is not to say you must be extroverted; there are plenty of introverted customers who are often more comfortable with introverted salespeople. As long as you are genuine in who you are, you can make sales. You'll be meeting people where they're at, with all of their imperfections, flaws, and insecurities, so learn to take the bad with the good. If you love making meaningful connections with other people, you will excel in sales and expand your network. You'll be invited to weddings, barbeques, parties. You name it! My holiday card list is quite a production after so many years of connecting with customers.

ENGAGING PEOPLE

You may have heard that sales is an art or that there is a science to selling. I believe both are true. Sales is like art in that it's creative. The artist (or salesperson) has excellent latitude on how they approach an opportunity to sell. I've seen innovative sales approaches, some resemble paintings and others sculptures. No sale is ever the same. Sales is also a science. It is observable, quantifiable, and experimental. You get to test hypotheses and develop conclusions to base future sales on. You have to approach deals with both an artist's creativity and a scientist's tools.

The most significant variable in selling is people. The best salespeople learn a lot about their customers and how to interact with them. However, all the education and training can't prepare you for the multitude of scenarios you will encounter with others. At the time of this book, there are 7.8 billion people on the planet, all with different histories, cultures, values, dreams, and experiences. Become comfortable with the fact that you'll never be fully prepared because of the unpredictability of the people you sell to. This chapter will give you ways to manage unpredictability.

Build Trust

Working with people, you need to establish trust quickly and naturally. We live in a world where trust is increasingly rare. Social media presents false images, identity, and data theft occur at alarming rates, and phishing spammers exploit your trust. This makes establishing trust in business even more difficult yet imperative. Trust between a customer and salesperson is one of the most effective tools for combating human unpredictability. It takes time to develop trust, and it can evaporate in seconds.

It only takes a moment for your customer to decide on their impression of you, but establishing lasting trust is a longer process. You can develop a positive impression of someone at your first meeting but fail to build trust. Think of trust on a continuum: when you first meet a prospective customer, don't expect to immediately gain their trust. You must continuously demonstrate integrity and quality of character. Over time they will come to trust you. The essence of who you are comes through during your sales, so you need to consistently hold yourself to the highest personal and professional standards.

Research has determined that trust is composed of three elements: predictability, dependability, and faith.[21] Develop predict-

---

21   John K. Rempel, John G. Holmes, and Mark P. Zanna, "Trust in close relationships," *Journal of Personality*

ability by avoiding surprises and sticking to your routine. Dependability means showing up when it matters. Keep your appointments, call when you say you will, and follow through on what you've committed to. Your customer will begin to have faith in you when you can consistently deliver on your promises and help fulfill their needs. Establishing yourself as trustworthy is so rare in sales that you will distinguish yourself as unique in a crowded field, setting you up for repeat business, up-sells, referrals, and long-lasting relationships.

Ken Blanchard, the celebrated author of *The One Minute Manager*, wrote an excellent parable on trust. *Trust Works* explains Ken's "ABCD Trust Model," an excellent process for establishing customer trust.[22] Here's how it works:

➤ **Ability**: You must have the ability, talents, and skills to help your customer through your sale.

➤ **Believability**: You need strong credentials, mutual respect, and a non-judgemental attitude. Show vulnerability, admit to your mistakes and be self-aware.

➤ **Connectedness**: Be present, easy to contact, and responsive to client needs. Show up with your full self, listen, and empathize.

➤ **Dependability**: Do what you say you're going to do when you say you're going to do it.

If you follow these tips for establishing trust with your customer, you'll be able to combat some of the unpredictability of working with

and Social Psychology 49, no. 1 (1985): xx, doi:10.1037/0022-3514.49.1.95.

22   Ken Blanchard, Cynthia Olmstead, and Martha Lawrence, *Trust Works!: Four Keys to Building Lasting Relationships* (New York: HarperCollins, 2013)

people and establish stronger client relationships.

Create Meaningful Connections

When you build a genuine connection with a customer, the likelihood they will buy from you increases, and you're able to combat the challenges of erratic human behavior. While selling relies on creating meaningful connections, those are more difficult to create today than ever before.   In the age of E-commerce, your customers can choose to shop online and get their product by the next day, all without ever engaging with an actual salesperson. That also makes true connection more important than ever before. To establish deeper connections you must understand:

1. Your customers and prospects were doing something meaningful before your call, not waiting with bated breath for a salesperson to contact them.

2. The internet enables your customers to research you, your company, your products and solutions, your competition, and your customers before you meet them.

3. You and your customers are strangers at first, so you must earn the right to ask questions and pique their interest. You can't break straight into your spiel about your company, product, or business opportunity. They won't care about that unless you connect with them as people first.

Later, chapters will be devoted more fully to connecting with people, but for now, I'll leave you with two essential tips to help you build relationships:

> **Listen actively**: Listening actively, with empathy, is an important part of building meaningful relationships. Listening eagerly and openly will teach you more about your customers and build deep connections.

> **Develop commonality**: When you listen actively and observe nonverbal cues, you're likely to find something in common with your customer. Perhaps you share a hometown, alma mater, or life experience. Find it and connect over it.

Learn Why People Buy

Do you know why people buy from you? Do you take time after the sale to ask customers why they chose you over the competition? Have you developed a feedback system to capture this information? When customers buy from you, especially early in a new business venture, it is crucial to ask *why*. Learn how to recreate your success. Effective selling is all about repetition, and you can't understand what's working if you can't track it. Create opportunities for clients to provide feedback and then track these insights.

CRM systems allow you to create reports and examine metrics tracking your sales. Over time, you will find patterns that reveal what is valuable to your past customers and likely critical to future customers as well. The more you know, the better off you will be as you learn to convert sales to insights, insights to actions, and actions to profits. Your ability to decode your customer's professional and personal motivations will unlock more in-depth levels of insight into why they chose to buy from you and how you can approach customers with similar motivations.

There is a lot of research into why people buy. Some of the reasons include: fear (think about COVID-driven sales), utility, reciprocity, replacement, indulgence, compassion, conservation, addiction, pleasure, and pain avoidance. Sometimes people buy for social issues, out of a sense of belonging, for ego gratification, or to bolster their identity with a target group.

There are many reasons why people buy, but the foundational truth is that people buy from you when your values are in alignment. It's that simple. The greater the value alignment with your customer, the more likely you are to successfully close the sale. Knowing why people buy from you, allows you to repeat successful strategies and predict the unpredictable more accurately.

Learn Why People Don't Buy

Just like knowing why your customers buy from you helps predict consumption behavior better, knowing why people *don't* buy from you is equally useful. It's productive to conduct loss reviews to discover what your customers valued, where you went wrong, and what other options they chose.

One of the most important steps when seeking feedback from customers who didn't go with your solution is to remove all judgment. Maintaining objectivity can be hard, but it's critical to stay impartial and non-emotional. These interactions are golden opportunities to learn about your mistakes, misunderstandings, and miscommunication. The customer is giving you the gift of feedback, and you should respond humbly and gratefully.

I missed an opportunity 20 years ago to get feedback from a customer who chose to go with a competitor. After a highly competitive fight for the sale, the customer called me and said, "I want to tell you how much we enjoyed working with you. However, we decided to go with your competitor. We do like you better, and I wish your solution met our needs." He told me our competitor added greater value than our solution did. I was too young and surprised to ask for more information, and should have asked him to elaborate so I could provide feedback to my company. I didn't and missed a perfect opportunity for growth.

So why don't people buy from you? It's usually a case of misaligned values, or lack of control. Sales are complicated, and people often make decisions that defy reason. It's important to remember that everyone has unique personal, positional, and organizational needs. Any small miscommunication of your product's value can tank a sale in a marketplace with a wealth of options. When you break down sales success and failure across multiple products, contexts, industries, and environments, you inevitably see misalignment of value and lack of control as recurring themes for failure.

Right now, you may be thinking, "He hasn't even mentioned price!" Pointing to price alone as a reason for a failed sale is simplistic and incorrect. How much someone is willing to spend depends on value alignment and control. It doesn't rely on the price by itself, ever. When you buy online, you may think you are buying solely on price. Let's take two items with the same price but different suppliers. Why do you choose one over the other? Shipping times? Your value alignment with the company? Think about why people choose to spend money at Starbucks when they can make a similar cup of coffee for less. It's based on value alignments like convenience, speed, and quality. Price is rarely a reason by itself; it all traces back to value alignment and control. Understanding how these factors shape your customers' decision whether or not to buy from you will help you prepare for their behavior.

Study People

So far we've seen that people are the one unpredictable factor that accounts for variability in selling, and we looked at ways to manage this. You can control a sale, but not the customer; people are unpredictable and don't like to be told what to do. This is why it's so important to be a student of human behavior.

Studying the people around you will provide helpful insights into their decision-making processes, values, and needs. Every sales research study emphasizes that the top two skills for effective selling are communication skills and listening skills. Engaging with your customers and actively listening to what they have to say will clue you in to what makes them tick. To understand human behavior further, analyze interpersonal competence in all your critical interactions. Studying interpersonal competence involves evaluating the quality of an interaction between two or more people and will help you understand effective communication. High levels of interpersonal competence lead to positive outcomes.[23] In addition to studying communication, you will benefit from researching negotiation, persuasion, psychology, and neuroscience, among others. There are many articles, books, and lectures to study in your free time, and learning the science behind human behavior will help you prepare for the unpredictability of your customers.

BARRIERS TO COMMUNICATION

You've learned that you need to communicate well in order to understand your customers, which will help you manage their unpredictability. In this section, you'll learn about the variety of barriers to

---

23   Spitzberg, B. H., & Cupach, W. R. (2002). Interpersonal skills. In M.L. Knapp, & J.A. Daly (Eds)., *Handbook of interpersonal communication* (3rd Ed. pp. 564-611). Thousand Oaks, CA: SAGE.

effective communication and how to overcome them. Communication barriers you're likely to encounter include:

> **Physical**: This may seem like a simple barrier, but it will completely shut down communication if not addressed. If you can't physically communicate with your customer, you are dead in the water. Imagine trying to sell to someone in a crowded room. You wouldn't be nearly as effective as if you were alone in your office. And in our age of virtual communication, you'll experience physical barriers such as slow network speed, video distortion, audio pops, reverberation, and lack of access to technology. Physical barriers can be overcome with straight-forward problem-solving. Leave the room if it's crowded, and ask for IT support if your web conference isn't working. Be proactive and don't wait for someone else to solve your problem for you.

> **Language**: This can be a significant barrier when it comes to international sales. If you can't communicate with your customer because you speak different languages, you'll need to immediately find a translator. Even if you speak the same language, you may find yourself running into problems. Regional and cultural differences in how words are used may mean your customer may not assign the same meaning to certain words as you do. Miscommunication can quickly derail a sale, so it's important to be clear and consistent in your language and regularly check that your customer is on the same page.

> **Cultural differences**: Cultural differences can lead to a breakdown in communication. Traditions and expecta-

tions vary across cultures. For instance, some cultures have a more rigid sense of time than others. Native American cultures have a circular concept of time instead of a linear one, meaning things happen in seasons, and there is a lack of finality. Researching cultural cues and potential differences before you engage with your customer will help keep communication on track.

> **Situational**: Situational barriers can seriously impede communication. For example, imagine selling to a client who is undergoing a crisis. It's important to know about crisis communication because you can choose to shut down communication channels, but that does nothing to shut down communication. Your customer still has needs, and you need to work with them to find the best way to communicate about how you can assist. They likely won't exhibit the behavior patterns you expected, and may be more volatile than you anticipated. I sold to customers who were significantly impacted by Hurricane Katrina in New Orleans, Louisiana. Some had lost loved ones, homes, and jobs. Their situation called upon my team to be empathetic and purposeful in our communication. Fast forward to today, when every company on the planet has to deal with the implications of the COVID-19 pandemic. It's changing how we communicate. You can't prepare for every possibility, so be ready to appraise the situation and roll with the punches.

Understanding the common communication barriers will help you adapt and prepare for the challenges of unpredictability.

CHOOSING THE RIGHT MEDIUM

In today's fast-paced world, we have a myriad of communication choices at our disposal. As a seller, especially during the pandemic, transitioning and utilizing all mediums of communication is essential. Resist the urge to believe the way things are now is the way they will always be. Innovation happens quickly, and sellers need to keep pace with changing mediums of communication. Choosing the right medium will allow you to connect better with your customers and keep up with their needs.

There are two types of communication to understand: direct and mediated communication. Direct communication involves upfront, in-person engagement. The interaction is face-to-face and synchronous – meaning in real-time. Mediated communication simply means there is a buffer (usually distance, technology, another individual, etc.) between you and the other person. The interaction can be synchronous or asynchronous. For instance, text messaging is asynchronous since you decide when you want to reply, if at all. On the other hand, video calls and conferencing are increasingly popular and offer synchronous, mediated interactions.

Even with all of these modern options, it can still be challenging to connect with people. Misattributing intent is a common problem with mediated communication, as it's easy to misinterpret a digital silence or delayed response. It's also easy to misuse a medium and negatively impact your seller-customer relationship. Sellers need to understand the arsenal of choices available to them, master each medium, and leverage the right communication tools at the right time. The proper medium will help you effectively communicate and connect with your client.

BELOW THE WATERLINE

As you grow and develop your sales career, you have to look below the waterline. If you've ever seen a boat, what's visible is above the waterline. To perform maintenance and repairs on the hull, you are required to dive deeper. I had a friend who lived on a superyacht in college who made his living scraping barnacles off the hull. Barnacles attach to the hull and damage the ship's efficiency when moving through the water; thus they need to be dealt with regularly.

This kind of maintenance is the same in sales. What lies below the waterline needs to be dealt with to make your journey to mutual value smooth and efficient. You need to periodically explore, challenge yourself to grow, and address weaknesses that may be difficult to acknowledge. If you exert effort, are committed to change, and are willing to put in the time to develop superior habits and patterns, you can soar to new heights. Getting below the waterline with your customers will also improve your understanding of their behavior.

What to look for below the waterline:

> **Fears**: We touched on this in Chapter 3, but examining your fears will free you up to overcome them. Recognize your customer has fears as well. I had a customer once tell me they didn't want to hurt my feelings. Examining the fears below the waterline will help you, and your customer increase your mutual confidence and improve your likelihood of a success-ful sale.

> **Empathic Inquiry**: This technique will help you gather more details from your customers. Ask questions such as, "How do you feel about this solution?" or "How has this process been for you?" These questions are designed to check

in with your customers and see if they are still comfortable. Such questions are effective in helping customers align with your value. Encourage the dialogue to help you get below the waterline. You should be open to asking for a status report, which will guide you to greater alignment.

> **Objections**: Objections are customer signposts to inform you that you and the customer are misaligned. Don't take them personally. Objections are gold nuggets to be mined and converted into cash. Whatever your customer says is real and valid for them. You don't want your customer to tell you what they think you want to hear. Instead, you want them to communicate issues out loud so you can jointly explore whether your product is the right solution for them. Seek clarity about their objections, and don't be afraid to solicit their no. For example, you might ask an objecting customer, "Help me understand your position here. I heard you say you believe our price is too high. Was that based on the total cost of the solution or just the initial cost of acquisition?" A question like this seeks to clarify their objection so you can help.

> **Silence**: When you get below the waterline, you'll find yourself dealing with information inherent to the customer's organization. Feel fortunate they trust you enough to share, and listen eagerly. Be silent and ask questions such as "Can you tell me more?" and "What else?" Encourage your customer to share their reality with you. Ask open-ended questions and make time to hear their answers. Practice silence and actively listen.

> **Biases**: Identify your biases and challenge them. If you are

looking to explore bias in yourself, I recommend looking at Harvard University's Project Implicit®, at implicit.harvard. edu, a collaboration among researchers into implicit social cognition. Psychologists Amos Tversky and Daniel Kahneman developed cognitive bias theory in the 1970s to illustrate how people process information. Tversky and Kahneman discovered that people move toward their preconceptions, a phenomenon they dubbed "confirmation bias," and proved these biases can result in illogical and irrational decision making.[24] A great antidote to bias is gaining more life experience. Look at the world through the lenses of others. Looking at the sale through your customer's lens will challenge your preconceptions as a seller and improve mutual value alignment.

Looking beneath the waterline will help both you and your customer communicate and connect on a deeper level.

TRAVEL IS A GIFT

Selling has to do with people, so how well do you know people? How often have you broken away from your little bubble to experience what others experience? Getting more familiar with others' backgrounds and experiences is part of what travel can do for you. You don't have to go anywhere dramatic. Traveling within your county is just as valuable. Trips don't have to be expensive. Just get going. Get in your car and drive. Book a trip to somewhere new and meet great people. Get off the beaten path and explore.

When you travel, you learn about different cultures, histories,

---

24   John Kidd et al., "Judgement under Uncertainty: Heuristics and Biasses," *The Journal of the Operational Research Society* 34, no. 3 (1983): xx, doi:10.2307/2581328.

and norms. If you have an opportunity to live and work in another country, take it. It will seem odd at first, but you will experience the beauty of another country and culture.

I lived in Germany and loved it. I lived above my landlord, who invited me into his home for Weihnachten, or Christmas celebrations. When I entered his house, I immediately noticed the sweet smell of spiced cookies and wine and was shocked to see candles burning on a real Christmas tree. I asked him, "Won't the whole house burn down?" feeling more than a little worried about my belongings upstairs. He laughed and explained that was how Germans have been celebrating for longer than the US has existed. He invited me to have some Gluwein.

You will find a wide range of diversity in your travels. Travel inspires us to learn about each other and provides a unique window to understanding others. Celebrating with my landlord opened up a new world to me. I loved how the Germans celebrate Weihnachten so much that I took my wife there to experience it herself. Our Christmas tree each year is decorated with remnants of the people and places we love to visit. It's always a joy to set it up each year and remember what we love about our travels, and think about where we want to explore next.

In business numerous faux-pas can occur when people take their workstyle to a new country or culture and fail miserably. American management is different from Japanese management, and a whole host of other countries as well. Take Walmart, for instance.[25]

In the US, we sell our food with expiration dates prominently displayed. However, in some Asian countries, they perceive this to mean the food is old and will not purchase items like this. Walmart

---

25   Walmart in China: Dramatically different than in the U.S. (2014, January 18). *The American Genius*. https://theamericangenius.com/business-news/walmart-china-dramatically-different-u-s/

and many other companies learned about the cultures of different countries and adjusted their approaches accordingly.

Taco Bell is another company that, in its global expansion, has sought to redefine the taco. Initially, this was problematic for the chain. However, if you visit anywhere in the world today, you will quickly see they have adapted the menu to include Banurittos, fresh bananas coated with Nutella® and wrapped in a flour tortilla with chocolate sauce (in Cyprus), or a Kimchi Quesadilla (Korea).[26] Coca-Cola produces many colas for markets worldwide, and even energy production companies have learned to take cultural considerations into mind, allowing time for siesta and prayer.

If you want to share in more of life, you have to commit yourself to travel. You will meet incredible people, see raw and rare beauty, learn history from another vantage point, and know yourself better. You can never travel too much. If you plan to travel to new and different locations, you will find it helps you become more open and approachable at the sales table.

My wife has the gift of being approachable. It seems people will come right up to her and start talking, sometimes revealing very personal information after meeting her for merely a few minutes. She is approachable in other countries too. I've been married to her for almost 25 years. It still amazes me how people approach and connect with her in seconds. Maybe you know people with a similar trait. What is it about these people that makes them so approachable? In the next chapter, we will dive deeper into how you can learn to be more approachable and develop that quality in your own life.

---

26 "12 Global Taco Bell Items That Will Give You Food Envy," FOODBEAST Food News, Videos and Recipes, accessed November 8, 2020, https://www.foodbeast.com/news/taco-bell-around-the-world/.

CHAPTER SUMMARY/KEY TAKEAWAYS

In this chapter, you learned:

> **People are unpredictable**: No matter how air-tight your sales plan is, people are unpredictable, and you may lose sales you thought would be slam dunks.

> **Engaging people**: Learn how to engage people to succeed in sales.

> **Build trust**: Establish rapport and develop trust as soon as possible.

> **Connect**: Build meaningful connections by showcasing your genuine self.

> **Learn why your customers buy**: Study what has made you successful in the past and what consumers want.

> **Learn why they don't buy**: Ask for feedback to understand how to overcome customer objections.

> **Study people**: Become a student of human behavior. The more you understand people, the better you can sell with them.

> **Communication barriers**: Many barriers may impede productive communication, including physical, linguistic, cultural, and situational.

> **Choose the right medium**: Ensure successful connections by choosing the appropriate communication form for your customer.

> **Get deeper**: Get to know your customers on more than a surface level by exploring their fears, engaging in empathic inquiry, discussing their objections, practicing golden silence, and challenging your biases.

> **Travel**: Travel more to expand your horizons, learn about different people and cultures, and gain new perspectives.

This chapter has addressed how to manage the most important and unpredictable aspect of your sale: People. Now that you know how to listen to and connect with your customers let's take a look at what you have to offer them.

WHAT DO YOU BRING TO THE PARTY?

It's possible you chose sales because it's a rewarding and lucrative career. Unfortunately, thousands of other people realized the same thing. There are a myriad of competing sales reps out there selling identical products as you, and it's harder than ever to set yourself apart from the rest. So how do you make an impression on your customer and stand apart from the rest?

You typically try to bring something unique when you attend a potluck, like a favorite dish, appetizer, drink, salad, dessert, etc. You wouldn't bring a bag of chips to a cookout when that's what everyone else is bringing. Bring something valuable, unique, and interesting, and you're sure to be invited back. Sales calls are no different.

What you bring to your sales meetings has the potential to set you apart from the competition. You can rely on the same logic that you follow at potlucks. What unique value can you add, beyond the deal you're offering, to help you close the sale? This chapter will help you realize your unique value.

In this chapter, you will explore the intangibles you bring to the selling environment. I'll show you how to use them to drive sales.

The skills you'll learn are backed by research in psychology, sociology, communication, organizational behavior, and neuroscience. First, you'll learn to present a well-prepared image to your customers. Then we'll talk about the value of bringing persuasive stories to your interactions. You'll learn about the Six People involved in interpersonal interactions, followed by how to leverage pre-communication. Finally, we'll talk about your brand and what it brings to the room.

PREPPING THE PERFECT IMAGE

The first step to make sure you are bringing unique value to your sales meetings is to improve your image. Put effort into your image to ensure your customer's first impression is a good one. If a picture is worth a thousand words, imagine the impact your image has on your client. Here are a few tips for presenting the best image possible:

> **Respect others' time**: No matter who you're selling to, respect their time. Be prompt and arrive at your meeting with plenty of time to spare. In the world of digital interaction, plan your schedule to take technology mishaps into account. Never show up late to a meeting: every minute you're late communicates to your customers that you don't value their time. You add the value of dependability to your customers' lives when you can be relied upon to show up promptly.

> **Physical appearance**: How you dress and manage your basic hygiene are simple cues telling your customer how much you value yourself. The expected level of formality changes with each meeting, but make sure your dress is appropriate, and you look put together. It will project a confident, capable image.

➤ **Lead with respect**: Mohammed Ali once said that he pays close attention to how people treat others, using it as an indicator for their character.[27] As I've said before, be nice to everyone. The minute you walk in the door, treat everyone with respect and dignity. You never know if the person you're talking to in the elevator has a huge influence over the future of your sale!

➤ **Smile**: It's a simple tip, but it communicates openness and ease. Your customers will be more comfortable and feel ready to open up to you when you adopt an approachable expression and demeanor.

➤ **Engage**: Resist the urge to disengage, check your phone, or otherwise get distracted. Today's technology pulls you into a world of constant communication, updates, and alerts. Silence your devices in meetings and stay fully present and engaged. Look at the other person in their eyes. And don't multitask during virtual meetings. Your customer can tell! Staying engaged will demonstrate to your customers that you value their time.

Use these tips to craft an image that your customers will respond positively to. When you bring an excellent image to the meeting, your customers will be more trusting and inclined to buy from you.

SELLING THE STORY

One of the best assets you can bring to the table to set you apart is a well-told, persuasive story. Sales can be very quantitative and

27   Liles, M. "Need some motivation? These 125 inspiring quotes from boxing legend Muhammad Ali are here to help." Parade: Entertainment, Recipes, Health, Life, Holidays. Last modified October 22, 2020. https://parade.com/1105459/marynliles/muhammad-ali-quotes/.

metrics based, and taking a break from the numbers to tell a narrative will set you apart from your competitors. When telling a story, it's essential to understand your audience. For example, executives care about hearing stories that relate to the significant drivers of company health. If you're selling to a CEO, make sure your story discusses profits, shareholder value, and revenue growth. Senior executives want to hear how your product aligns with their company's strategic goals, so work this into your story. Line of business executives will care more about process, so stories about cycle times and customer service will be attractive to them.

Once you've tailored your story to your audience, find appropriate evidence to support your narrative. Evidence is the glue that ties your story together, and good evidence has recency, authority, and alignment. Let's look at these in turn:

> **Recency**: Your evidence must be timely. In today's fast-paced world, customers only want to hear about what will give them an advantage *now*. They don't care about the story of how a company succeeded 30 years ago. Putnam Investments used to have an ad that said, "You think you understand the situation, but what you don't understand is that the situation just changed." Our business world changes at a rapid pace, and if your story isn't relevant in the moment you tell it, your audience won't care

> **Authority**: Give your audience a reason to trust your evidence. Research who they consider to be an authority in their industry and include evidence from such authoritative figures. If you're selling to a CEO, for instance, they likely trust other CEOs. Look at the world from their perspective to understand who they look up to, then utilize evidence

from these authorities.

> **Alignment**: Your evidence should align with the industry you're selling in. Don't force your customers to make the connection to the potential sale themselves. Clearly spell out how this story applies to your professional relationship.

SIX PEOPLE

Up to this point we've explored how you can control what *you* bring to the party. But you aren't the only one showing up. According to Dean Barnlund, a pioneer in human communication research, there are *six people* involved in every interpersonal interaction.[28] These people are a metaphor for the different perspectives and intuitions at play in any communicative situation. Getting to know these people will help you understand the invisible elements you bring to the party and how to leverage them. The six people include:

1. How you view yourself
2. How you view the other person
3. How you think the other views you
4. How you think the other person views themselves
5. How the other person views you
6. How the other person believes you view them

How well you know these six people will determine your interpersonal success. Let's just take the first one as an example. How do you see yourself? Do you have a positive self-image? This impacts the

---

28 Stephen W. Littlejohn and Karen A. Foss, *Theories of Human Communication* (Boston: Cengage Learning, 2008)

third person: how you think your customer views you.

Communication is contextual, and your perceptions of your customer and theirs of you will significantly impact your relationship. It's essential to check in with these six people to see how they may be subconsciously influencing your actions. You bring them with you to every party, so you need to keep in tune with them.

PRE-COMMUNICATION

Before you even get to the party, you can leverage tools of pre-communication to make sure your client perceives you as offering something unique and valuable. Pre-communication is what people come to believe about you in advance of your planned interactions. Here are some research studies illustrating the effect of pre-communication.

In one study it was pre-communicated to participants that they would meet either a very tall individual or a very short one. When participants were later asked about the person's height, the results were clear. They believed the heights were what had been pre-communicated to them, even though all the subjects were the same height.

Another study involved elementary school teachers who heard pre-communicated information about which students were smart before meeting their classes. The pre-communicated messages caused teachers to spend more time and attention with the kids they thought were smart, and less with the others.

With this in mind, what might you do to influence your customers? What information could you pre-communicate to convince your customers that you add value to their businesses and lives? Match your language to their values, and encourage your customers to see you as someone who brings a lot of unique value to the party.

WHAT'S YOUR BRAND?

Brands aren't only for companies. To be a successful salesperson you'll want to develop an airtight and recognized personal brand. To start, conduct research to discover how others currently perceive your brand. You can create formal surveys, ask for direct feedback, and look at your social media engagement. A good way to think about your brand is to ask what you are known for. Do people identify you with expertise in a particular area, an ability to get things done, creativity, or some other valuable quality? Alternate the tactics you use to learn about your brand to get a fuller and more honest picture.

What happens if you don't like your brand? Change it. People change their brands and reinvent themselves every day. It takes dedication and focused attention, but improving your brand perception is an investment in yourself as a salesperson that helps you bring more to the table.

Set a brand goal that will help you bring more to your customers. Consider aiming for a brand of professionalism, dependability, leadership, accountability, or something similar. When you establish a popular, trusted brand for yourself your customers will believe that you bring a lot of value to the party.

CHAPTER SUMMARY/KEY TAKEAWAYS

In this chapter, you learned:

> **What do you bring to the table?**: You have to bring something unique to the party. Wow your customers by demonstrating how you can add unique value to their lives.

> **Perfect your image**: Take care to present yourself as respectful, positive, and engaging to show your customers that you add value.

> **Sell the story**: Use persuasive storytelling to bring more to the table, and rely on recency, authority, and alignment when choosing your evidence.

> **Six people**: You bring more than yourself to the party. Get to know the "six people" involved in every situation to help you show up more fully.

> **Pre-communication**: Utilize strategic pre-communication to positively influence your client's perception of your value in advance.

> **Find your brand**: Solicit feedback on your brand and then strive to develop a professional, capable, reliable reputation. Your brand itself will help you add value to the room.

Now that you know how to bring more to the party, we're going to dive back into the nitty-gritty of the sales industry. The next chapter will teach you how to be an effective sales manager or work with an ineffective one.

SALES MANAGERS SUCK

Nurturing healthy, professional relationships can be complicated in a highly competitive industry like sales. This chapter will teach you how to improve your salesperson-manager relationship. If you work for a difficult sales manager, the next section will walk you through a technique for getting rid of excuses and breaking down your mental barriers. Then, you will study five everyday situations caused by bad managers and learn how to overcome them. The following section will address the relationship from the sales manager's side and teach you six important attributes necessary to become a stellar manager. Finally, you will learn the value of expanding your network beyond the seller-manager relationship, and I'll show you how to do it.

YOUR SALES MANAGER DOESN'T SUCK

Managers are the number one reason why salespeople stay with a company. They are also the biggest reason why salespeople leave a company. But the problem isn't your manager. It's your perception of your manager. For instance, even top-performing salespeople rarely cite their managers as a reason they sell more. Most salespeople don't respect their managers. They feel their manager doesn't do anything to help them or make some other excuse. Yup – I said it. Excuse! You probably have a laundry list of excuses about your manager holding you back right now. Here are some of the ones I've heard frequently. Go ahead and circle the ones you identify with. If you don't see one of your favorites on the list, add it in:

1. My manager set my quota too high and expects too much, especially in this economy.

2. My manager didn't provide adequate training.

3. My manager overworks me.

4. I'm not provided with enough resources.

5. I'm going through personal struggles, and my manager isn't accommodating.

6. My manager assigned me a problematic territory.

These are not worth what you are making of them! You can make a million different reasons not to do something, but in the end your mind is what's holding you back. You've convinced yourself that you'll never succeed because of an external force: your manager. But in reality, you've internalized excuses. Until you get past your mental obstacles, you'll flounder. It's time to retrain your mind and change your outlook.

You may think I'm being harsh, but I've worked for sales leaders who had no business in their positions, gave bad advice, and did everything to chip away at my confidence. Too many companies today promote leaders from unrelated business units and make them sales managers without ever asking them to sell. They seem to assume anyone with an MBA can sell, and they fail to train new managers. I believe that, at a minimum, every sales leader should go through the same training their employees go through and experience front line sales so they understand the salesperson's perspective.

I know from experience there are more bad managers than good, but how you ultimately respond is entirely your choice. You are the one responsible for managing yourself. This chapter will help you refocus your energy so you can handle any situation.

(There is one situation I don't want to mince words on – and that is abuse. If you are in an abusive workplace situation, please contact your HR team or the police immediately. It's intolerable and illegal.)

OVERCOMING DIFFICULT MANAGERS

Truly great salespeople learn how to navigate barriers, even when those barriers are the people who are supposed to be helping you. You come up against a million obstacles in life, and if you give up easily you'll never be successful. In this section, you'll learn how to overcome the barrier of a difficult manager.

Approach the relationship with your manager similar to the way you would approach a demanding customer. For instance, if you create call plans for your customers, why not make one for inter-actions with your boss? Sell them on your competence, skills, and ideas. Even top performers must do this. Each day provides a new set of opportunities to impress management and move forward. I've spent years coaching people through negative employee-manager rela-tionships and will show you how to overcome them in this section. Let's dive into some common scenarios.

My Way or the Highway

Sally was an extraordinary account executive, known for high customer satisfaction and sales achievement. So when a new sales manager job opened up, everyone wanted to see Sally take the next step into management. However, there wasn't much consideration of what made Sally effective or whether there might be an alternative career path that would make more sense based on her skillset. Sally was chosen based on the belief that sales careers are linear and that a rep should follow a path up to management.

Trouble arose about four months after Sally moved into her new role when two-long time performers quit on the same day, citing their displeasure with Sally as their manager. When HR dug deeper, they learned that Sally was quick to show her displeasure when her team wasn't following her instructions to the letter. One of her salespeople never used presentation software, preferring to have 1:1 conversations and whiteboarding discussions. Sally was opposed to this alternative approach and chastised her sellers for not doing things exactly her way.

How do you approach this type of overbearing sales manager? What is the right way to get them to appreciate the validity of your approach? First, listen carefully to their feedback. This type of manager wants to be heard and validated. When they share, respond authentically, "I love that idea. You're right, and I can see how that's been successful for you. What about my approach did you appreciate? What elements are similar to yours?" It's then essential to highlight your approach's positive outcomes and communicate how your way was equally effective in achieving the desired result. Focus on results with this manager while continuing to validate and learn from their perspective.

Nothing is Ever Good Enough

There is nothing worse than working for a perfectionist. While their intent is honorable, they quietly erode the confidence and swagger of their sellers by convincing them that nothing will ever be good enough to win their praise. As a result, employees stop trying to stand out and settle on mediocrity.

What should you do as a salesperson working under a manager like this? Be thankful for the opportunity and prepare to learn. Look to your perfectionist boss for clues about how they want you to work. If you're confused about what's important to them, it's important to ask. If they have a myriad of KPI's, ask them to rank them. This will help you discern what is most valuable. Then look for what they do well and compliment them. In Jeffrey Fox's book titled *How to Become CEO*, Fox suggests that you find ways to help your boss look good and ways to make your boss's boss look good.[29] Be authentic and try to find the good in what your boss is doing. Cultivating a positive relationship is a two-way street.

This may sound overly simplistic, but it has been an influential mantra throughout my career: Do your best. Early in my sales career I found myself working for a small startup that was able to land a huge deal with IBM. Our CEO, Edward, put me in charge of leading the sales effort and coordinating our request for proposal (RFP) response. This was the most significant opportunity in my life up to this point, and I put everything I had into it. I worked with our team nonstop, working overtime to research our competition, calling IBM, talking with our software engineers, and consulting our partners. I wrote for hours every day to craft a new proposal but struggled to overcome the doubts and second-guessing swirling

---

29   Jeffrey J. Fox, *How to Become CEO: The Rules for Rising to the Top of Any Organization* (New York: Hachette Books, 2001)

around in my head.

Every few days, I'd bring Edward a new RFP. He always reacted the same way, taking one glance at the cover page before throwing it down in disgust. Each time I asked myself, *what can we improve here?*

Then I'd go spend more time talking with our team, customers, and IBM. Each draft improved my confidence, and after about 18 different revisions, I took the RFP response once again to Edward. This time, I marched into his office a little pissed off but confident we had done our *very best work*. I explained as much to Edward.

Edward paused and then said to me, "OK. Now I'll read it." I was dumbfounded. Hadn't he even been reading it? I was speechless, and it took some time for the lesson to sink in.

Edward taught me that I had to overcome my doubt before I could succeed. I also learned the importance of the TEAM principal (Together Everyone Achieves More) and challenged myself to push further. Then, when you have pushed your team to the brink of exhaustion, you are ready.

We won the business with IBM. It was one of the biggest wins in my career and a game-changer for our company. We hired more people and grew. We gained swagger. Edward was a perfectionist, and I could have let that deter me, but I used his high standards to push myself to a level I never thought possible, and that's what you must learn to do when you have sales managers who seem impossible to please.

Style vs. Substance

Another type of manager you might have is one who critiques you based on style points. Like the "my way or the highway" manager, this manager tends to be overly controlling and tries to micromanage your selling process, precisely your style. This manager likely wants you to represent the company in a specific way or thinks salespeople all need to stick to the same brand. It can be incredibly frustrating to work with a manager who critiques your style but ignores your stellar results. If you approach sales differently from your manager and your manager refuses to accept it, how do you then get past this style vs. substance barrier?

First, be open to learning a new way to get things done. Ask your sales manager for recommendations: "How have you seen others do this? Could you show me some new ways that might work?" Allow them to guide your style. Most importantly, try to shift your manager's focus to the outcome. Find opportunities to show them your stellar sales numbers and reassure them you're still succeeding, albeit with slightly different methods. Find a happy medium between adopting some of their suggestions and staying true to yourself.

Open vs. Directive Behavior

Some sales managers choose to direct their teams like a general in battle. Directive leaders bark commands: "Our pipeline sucks, fix it! Our sales are down. Improve them!" These managers have a clear sense of the desired outcome, but their directive behavior doesn't inspire or give clues on how to get such an outcome. If your manager were to open up, start a team conversation, and create a vision and sense of direction, they would likely get better results. But good luck convincing a directive manager of that.

If you are a salesperson with a directive manager, try to move them towards being more open. Offer advice that is congruent with their stated direction. You could say, "I heard what you said about our pipeline. I'd like your support to organize a team to look into this. Can we count on your help to think through the causes and develop a plan to get us to our goal?" This provides your manager with the opportunity to engage in more open behavior. Some people are just wired to be directive leaders and need a little help opening up. By supporting their leadership while encouraging them to share their thought process, you work towards the desired outcome while establishing yourself as a reliable person your boss can count on.

Rational vs. Emotional

People are simultaneously rational and emotional. We rationalize our behavior based on how we see the world. It's how we make sense of things. We also respond emotionally to situations. While this is natural, it becomes a problem when sales managers don't have the right balance of emotion and rationality.

Some bosses are toxic and use emotion as a weapon. Many bosses try to use fear as a motivator by bullying their subordinates. While such tactics work to an extent, they can have devastating consequences on employee health and morale. According to the Workplace Bullying Institute, more than 60 million Americans are subject to workplace bullying, and their health, quality of life, and future at their company suffer.[30]

What can you do to deal with emotionally volatile bosses? It is essential to stop focusing on them and instead focus on your work. Set personal boundaries and rules on how you deserve to be treated. You don't have to endure their bad behavior. Deal with their outbursts by doing the opposite: walking away calmly. You can even say you don't wish to talk with someone unwilling to show you respect.

Next, start to collect a file of documents and notes about the abuse. Report it to someone above your boss and HR. Are there other targets for your boss's bad behavior? Create a network and encourage them to document their experiences. Together, at a minimum, you

---

30   accessed November 9, 2020, https://workplacebullying.org/#start.

may help your lousy boss get the help and coaching they need. Remember, bad bosses are people too. Any number of things could be going on. However, you don't need to accept a hostile work environment. Acquire the visibility and help you need to change it.

ATTRIBUTES OF EXCELLENT SALES MANAGERS

The second half of this chapter contains some tips for sales managers to learn how to be more effective in their roles. I've been in sales for nearly thirty years, and I know what it takes to lead. An ideal relationship between the sales leader and sales professional is similar to that of a coach and athlete. To find the recipe for success, I asked a hundred salespeople to share their best managers' traits. In this section managers will discover the qualities and skills necessary to coach and empower a high-performing team.

Understanding Personal Issues

It's easy to forget as a manager that your employees are people too. You can become so focused on the bottom line and with putting up great numbers that you forget to show your employees compassion. One of the most important things for a boss to do is show understanding when employees open up about struggles in their personal lives. It will help you to forge a stronger connection with them and offer support and resources. Addressing the root of the problem instead of critiquing a sub-par work performance will put you in a position to help your employees make lasting changes and improve both their personal and professional lives.

Here's an example: Tommy is late every day. He was one of your top salespeople, but recently his numbers have been slipping, and he's been setting a bad example for younger employees. Why can't

Tommy get his butt out of bed and get to work on time? You can either reprimand him or ask if everything is all right outside of work.

If you choose to reprimand Tommy without learning more, you may inadvertently add stress to his situation and cause him to shut down further. Instead, sit down with him. As a manager, stick to what you have observed without ascribing judgment. Seek to understand what is going on and be open to possibilities. Reference observable behavior, and then ask questions like, "Tommy, I've noticed you arriving late to work for the last few weeks. I'm interested to hear what is going on with you and understand how I can help."

Approaching your employee with a caring, open manner will invite honest dialogue and help you understand the situation. Perhaps Tommy will reveal that he recently went through a divorce and suddenly has sole custody of his daughter. He now has to drop her off at school each morning and struggle to make it on time afterward. Knowing this explains his behavior and puts you in place to work on a solution together. Maybe you'll suggest he works from home in the mornings or stays a bit later in the afternoon to account for lost time.

However you handle it, you've solved a problem using empathy and have won the respect and trust of your employee. Some of the best advice I ever received came from a former boss. He told me to remember that my sellers were all people. They all have hopes and dreams. Treat them with care.

Make Your Vision Contagious

Excellent sales managers must possess a unique, results-centered vision. Let everyone on the team know what your expectations are. Communicate the process, confirm progress along the pipeline, and coach your team to the win. Then go beyond these basic building blocks.

Articulate your vision so clearly that your team can taste it. Inspire them with regular motivational reminders of what you're collectively working towards, and paint a detailed picture of how success will look. Understand how your employees' dreams fit into your vision, and help them see how success will affect them all. Translate your ideal results into meaningful goals your team will want to chase.

Compete Fiercely

Consider great football coaches like Vince Lombardi, Bill Belichick, Tom Landry, Don Shula, and John Madden. You might immediately think of their big games, their passion, and their love of winning. With six Superbowl victories, Bill Belichick established a culture of winning at the New England Patriots. If you dig deeper, you see he learned from Bill Parcells and other great leaders. He also practiced discipline and tenacity, was intensely competitive and established a legacy.

Top sales managers are fiercely competitive. They conduct themselves with a winning attitude and hold themselves to a high ethical standard. Their salespeople feed off their energy and are infected with their passion for winning. When sellers are around competitive leaders, they unconsciously shape themselves in that image and become more driven and aggressive. Take these lessons to your team and establish an expectation for winning. Your best employees will appreciate it and be motivated by it. Those who are not are probably better suited elsewhere. When you set out to win, and do so with purpose and integrity, your team will follow.

Model Strong Integrity

As a sales manager, you're always being watched. This is why you need to make it a habit to practice integrity in everything you do. Integrity means doing the right thing and doing things right. It's keeping your word, standing up for fairness, and calling out injustice. When you model strong integrity, you foster trust and honesty within your team and are role models for others.

Integrity for a sales leader involves leading with your values and those of your company. What values are important to you and how can you conduct yourself to embody those? For instance, you may value your family, but how are you honoring this if you travel 90% of the time? When your values conflict with your actions, your word becomes worthless. Now, what if instead you take your family with you when you travel, or travel less? Now your values are in alignment and everyone believes you.

Another critical dimension of integrity is fair pay. I've seen companies that espouse fairness as a value but compensate their salespeople unjustly. Not surprisingly, their talented sellers are always leaving. Not only are you opening yourself up for lawsuits if you shortchange on commission, but you are not doing the right thing. Don't cheat your employees. When you compromise on your values, you can never go back. You erode confidence and morale in an instant. Lead with integrity, and your team will follow. Trust, honesty and communication will flourish, and performance will improve as a direct result.

Show Appreciation

Appreciation is one of the most important things to give your employees as a sales manager. Seek out and applaud the unique strengths each person brings to the job. If you have never taken personality tests, I recommend them. One of my favorites is Gallup's *Strengths Finder*.[31] Not only do these tests identify positive behavioral

31   https://www.gallup.com/cliftonstrengths/en/strengthsfinder.aspx

tendencies, they make you a better leader by also identifying areas for growth. As a leader it helps to know what you are good at, and what you should improve. Shore up your weaknesses by partnering with others who possess those strengths. Recognizing your weaknesses can help you be more effective at showing appreciation, as it makes it easier to recognize the gifts others bring to the potluck.

Some of your salespeople will be naturally gifted in presenting, but bad at negotiating. Some may be dashboard pilots who can enter everything into the CRM, but fall short in a meeting. Seeing people for who they indeed are is a skill. Learn to recognize employees for their unique gifts and talents. Affirm them for doing well, and they will do more of it.

Many companies consider talent easily replaceable, leading to a "what have you done for me lately" sales culture. This makes employees nervous that termination lurks around every corner, creating stress that holds them back from performing well. Now imagine infusing such a culture with active appreciation. You'll see people open up, trust increases, productivity rise, absenteeism decreases, and sales improve. Customers may become more satisfied, and complaints will decrease. It's incredible how your leadership impacts your business. Create a culture of appreciation, and it will pay dividends.

Be Authentic

Authenticity is in short supply. People want to work for a leader who displays a high degree of authenticity. To be authentic, you have to be vulnerable. There's a lot of putting on airs in sales, so genuine leaders are few and far between. In Texas we call grandstanding businessmen "all hat, no cattle." Inauthentic people use impression management to guard who they are and present a fabricated version of their identity to others. The best bosses are honest about their faults and proud of their strengths, and they make others feel safe to be authentic too.

Lorraine was a manager I admired for her authenticity and compassion. She persuaded me to pursue sales, helped promote me, and when I later decided to leave the company she encouraged me to chase my dreams. I still feel like if I approached her today decades later, she would give me a big hug and welcome me into her office. She exuded authenticity and genuine love for her people. I am indebted to her for how she modeled authentic leadership. She was always there to help. No issue was too big and no problem too complicated. She smiled often and spoke with conviction and care. I was blessed to have her as one of my first sales leaders. Thanks, Lorraine!

In my discussions with salespeople, authenticity was either the first or second trait everyone wanted in a sales manager. Being authentic as a sales leader is about owning up to your mistakes. When your team fails, take ownership. Don't make excuses. Look for ways you can help reduce your employees' burdens, not create more.

Being authentic means keeping people around you who are more than yes men and women. You need people who will tell you what your faults are. This helps you realize your potential and use your authenticity to inspire others to reach their potential. Be an advocate for your salespeople. Coach them, respect them, and hear them. Help them progress toward their dreams. Recognize their achievements and celebrate their successes. Realize when you have people who are better than you and promote them into new areas where they can grow. To be authentic means to live without fear, be open to new ideas, and be approachable.

DEVELOPING YOUR NETWORK

So far this chapter has addressed the manager-salesperson relationship from both sides, but this last section will show you how to expand your network beyond that relationship. If you don't have a solid network, the best time to start building one is today.

Networking is all about connecting and maintaining relationships. When you meet new people, think about ways to develop meaningful connections with them. Take time to learn about their interests and how you can help meet their needs. Keep in touch with people over the years, because you never know when you can help each other out! Recruiters are great people to include in your network, and can be especially helpful if you ever need to build a team or look for a new job. Make sure your relationship is a 2-way street by offering help whenever someone reaches out. This will build a stronger relationship and you'll know you can rely on them in the future.

Make sure to check in with your connections regularly, not just when you need something. Wish them a happy birthday each year, congratulate them for new positions, and check in over the holidays. I have someone in my network whom I will call Sheila. Sheila is a fun person, full of life, and always great to be around. However, I never hear from her unless she needs something, like a job recommendation. While I will help her when asked, I'd like to hear from her more often. Now, think for a moment – are you a Sheila in someone else's network?

I love LinkedIn, and not just because they are part of Microsoft. It's a great way to stay connected with your network. LinkedIn helps you remember birthdays, alerts you to job changes, and cues you in to what's happening in your network. Make it a point to visit the site every day.

Finally, think about how often you add to your network. How proactive are you in meeting new people? Make time to meet new people. You can network within clubs, service organizations, and formal events. In the era of COVID, you'll want to try to network virtually. Remember my advice for connecting with people? Greet, Relate, Question, Reflect! Be open and receptive to meeting new people in networking environments. Before you even enter the room, say to yourself, "I am excited to meet new people." Think for a moment about the lasting connections you may make and the new friends that await. Isn't it exciting? How might your life change in a matter of moments based on whom you might meet? So many of us are not open to the wonder and possibility of the world. Make time for building connections, be deliberate, and open yourself up. Seek to understand and unlock more about people as if they were a valuable vault filled with jewels and riches. If you believe in other people, you will discover the value inside of them.

CHAPTER SUMMARY/KEY TAKEAWAYS

In this chapter, you learned:

> **Professional relationships are challenging**: Whether you're a sales manager or salesperson, navigating this boss-employee relationship is challenging but critical to your success.

> **No more excuses**: You may think you have the worst manager in the world, but it's time for you to stop making excuses and start breaking down self-imposed barriers.

> **Handling difficult managers**: Here are the ways to approach different types of bad managers:

>> **My way or the highway**: Stay focused on results and remain open to trying things differently.

>> **Nothing is ever good enough**: Push yourself to do your very best.

>> **Style vs. Substance**: Accept that your manager may have a different style than yours, and learn to adapt.

>> **Open vs. Directive Behavior**: Provide opportunities for your manager to lead with open behavior.

>> **Rational vs. Emotional**: Counter an over-emotional boss by staying measured and calm. Advocate for yourself to HR if necessary.

> **Attributes of excellent managers**: Acquire these tools to become the best manager you can be:

>> **Understanding personal issues**: Remember your employees are human too. Try to understand what's going on with them behind the scenes.

>> **Make your vision contagious**: Let your vision infect your team and take you to new heights.

→ **Compete fiercely**: Model a winning, competitive attitude, and it will translate to your team.

→ **Model strong integrity**: Conduct yourself with honesty and fairness.

→ **Show appreciation**: Celebrate your team's strengths and use them to complement your own weaknesses.

→ **Be authentic**: Get in touch with your vulnerable self and let it take the lead.

➤ **Develop your network**: Work hard to develop meaningful connections with a variety of professionals, and you'll always have help when you need it.

Now that you understand how to handle the salesperson-manager relationship from both sides, let's move on and talk about something that's critical and difficult: Listening.

LISTEN UP

Most sales guides will tell you what to say, but in this chapter I'll teach you how to hear. Even if you think you have an airtight pitch, you might fumble your sale if you don't make space to listen to what your customer has to say to you. Steamrolling ahead without listening to your customer will cause you to miss key cues about what's important to them, their hesitations, and their goals. Without this information you'll never achieve value alignment. This is why listening well is your single biggest asset when it comes to selling. People fundamentally want to be understood, but many salespeople get so caught up pitching their latest whiz-bang widget that they don't stop to investigate whether their customers even want or need it in the first place.

You might think you have such a basic concept as listening mastered. Let's find out whether you do. Check off any of the following if you've done it during a customer or prospect meeting:

> ➤ Checked your email during the "dead space in the meeting"

> ➤ Interrupted someone

> ➤ Jumped to a solution without letting the prospect finish their thoughts

➤ Offered suggestions while a customer struggled to explain something

➤ Asked others to "get to the point"

➤ Caught yourself daydreaming

➤ Mentally prepared for your next meeting instead of focusing on the current one

It's unlikely you got through this list without checking off a few of these behaviors. It's all right. We're only human. This chapter will help you develop your talents as a superstar listener so you can make sure your clients are heard. First, you'll learn about bad listening habits. Then, I'll walk you through what it means to "actively" listen. Next we'll touch on "empathetic listening" to align you with your clients emotionally. Finally, you'll learn how to extend your newfound listening skills to the rest of your team.

WE'RE BAD AT LISTENING

How often have you been told in your life to "listen up" or "please listen to me?" If you're like me, it's a lot. People are bad listeners. This is because our brains like to create shortcuts. We can comprehend 800 words per minute, but we speak at just 125 words per minute. That leaves a lot of extra brainpower for daydreaming. Our brains filter out all the unnecessary "filler" to focus on the main points. We look for patterns based on our experiences, culture, and history.

With technology speeding up communication, listening is more important than ever. The average person today gets interrupted by alerts every two seconds. New emails, texts, and application alerts are constantly pinging in. We are constantly distracted by the din of devices.

Studies show the distractions of technology cause us to miss out on life. My grandmother believed this. She lived to be 105 years old and would tell me the thing that changed the most in her life was people. "It's a wonder more people don't die because everyone is looking at their little screens," she used to say.

When we spend so much time looking at our phones, we consequently spend less time looking at *each other*. Because of this, we have become increasingly uncomfortable with emotion, often rushing past it to deal with facts instead. Silence makes many jittery, so we rush to fill it up with meaningless chatter. But listening matters, as Harvard professor Dr. Francis Peabody taught his students. He emphasized that listening was vital to the future of medicine.[32] How you feel about your doctor likely has a lot to do with how well they listen to and understand you. Whether you're in medicine or sales, your customers want to be heard. The best way to meet that need is through active listening.

ACTIVE LISTENING

Understanding active listening helps to compare it to our natural listening state, passive listening. When we listen passively, we aren't focused on any one thing. Instead, we casually and ineffectively consume a range of information all at once. Think of trying to get work done while you have the baseball game playing in the background. Are you really focused? Probably not.

Active listening, on the other hand, involves intention. To do it, you have to consciously make an effort to listen. We often try to milk every moment from our days by scheduling back-to-back

32   FRANCIS W. PEABODY, "THE CARE OF THE PATIENT," *JAMA: The Journal of the American Medical Association* 88, no. 12 (1927): xx, doi:10.1001/jama.1927.02680380001001.

meetings. This leaves no time for thinking, reflecting, and process-ing what we heard during the previous meeting. Think for a minute about what you are communicating to the other people in a meeting when you rush from one meeting to the next. You belittle their time to another boring meeting and you diminish how valued they feel. You may even try to mask your failure to actively listen by practicing "display listening." Display listeners are active on today's web confer-ence calls and want everyone to believe they are listening, so they attentively nod and make eye contact. However, they are more likely to construct what they want to say next and will miss the meaning of what is presently being shared.

But why does active listening matter, and what's wrong with display listening? According to Pew Research, we are living in the most divisive time in history.[33] Millions of peoples' values are in conflict, and dialogue is breaking down. Harvard law professor Mary Ann Glendon noted this thirty-five years ago in her book *Rights Talk: The Impoverishment of Political Discourse.* She observed that our imagined and perceived "rights" were getting in our way of meaningful discussion. To end a conversation, all anyone has to do is talk about or assert their "rights." Glendon redirects us back to communicating with responsibility, accountability, and sociality to work towards shared understanding and civility. But to get to a point where we understand people, we have to listen to them. We can only solve problems together when we shut our mouths and open our ears.

Active listening helped me close an important deal early in my career. I was selling to a customer who shared what they liked about my solution, and what they liked about my competitor's. Their "ideal" solution would be to merge our teams. We had to choose – do we walk

---

33   "86% of Americans Say Conflicts Between Democrats, Republicans Are Strong," Pew Research Center, last modified August 18, 2020, https://www.pewresearch.org/fact-tank/2017/12/19/far-more-americans-say-there-are-strong-conflicts-between-partisans-than-between-other-groups-in-society/.

away from this deal, or keep pushing for the contract? We did neither. Instead we actively listened to the customer, understood what they wanted, and worked to build an alliance with our competitor.

There is a saying in sales that "pigs get fed, and hogs get slaughtered." It means, don't be a fool and let greed take hold. It calls for you to listen and adopt out of the box thinking to make the smart choice, even if it seems less profitable. The first time we proposed a partnership with our competitor, we were on thin ice and felt their distrust. But after long discussions and active listening, we decided that together we could give the customer exactly what they needed. The customer was thrilled we'd found a way to work together, and the result was one of the most fulfilling customer relationships of my career. It was an unordinary solution, grounded in listening.

Now that you understand what active listening entails and why it matters, it's time to learn how to become an active listener.

Plan to Focus

According to a recent study by Accenture, technology distracts and inhibits listening for 80% of people who multitask during meetings when they should be focused.[34] Active listening means creating an environment where you can focus solely on your customer. To plan for this, you must eliminate any distractions that compete for your focus. Turn off your phone, close your laptop, and set up for the meeting in a quiet, distraction-free location. Don't give gadgets the chance to steal the spotlight. Consume information on your own terms, not when an application decides to push out notifications. Examine your meeting habits to determine how they may be inadvertently causing you to lose focus. Perhaps you're an avid note-taker.

---

34 "Accenture Research Finds Listening More Difficult in Today's Digital Workplace," Newsroom | Accenture Newsroom, accessed November 8, 2020, https://newsroom.accenture.com/industries/global-media-industry-analyst-relations/accenture-research-finds-listening-more-difficult-in-todays-digital-workplace.htm.

While note-taking helps you remember key numbers, dates, and ideas, it also means you are distracted from your customer.

A good way to check in on your focus is to analyze why you're listening. According to Steven Covey, the famous author of *Seven Habits of Highly Effective People*, "we listen with the intent to reply, not to understand." One of his well-known recommended habits is "seek first to understand, then be understood."[35] Check-in on yourself to determine whether you are trying to understand the other person or trying to find an opportunity to step in. I'd challenge you to think through how you might take notes and simultaneously understand the other person. Active listening means you have to focus intently to hear. Listen for quotes instead of being focused on your notes.

Pay Attention

Once your mind is focused, pay attention! The biggest challenge here is to quiet your noisy mind and put your thoughts on hold. Tell yourself your mind is allowed to wander *after* the meeting. Paying attention becomes easier when you are open to the possibility of learning something new.

If you are in a position of authority, open yourself up to the possibility that you can learn something new from anyone, no matter their position. If you are running a company, pay attention to what the frontline workers tell you about your customers, supply chain, quality, and finances. If you are in a sales meeting, get excited to learn about your customer and how you might help them.

When you pay attention, fix your gaze on the other person and observe all the ways they communicate. How are they sitting? What expressions are on their face? Do they seem nervous or relaxed? Do

35   Covey, Stephen R. *The 7 Habits of Highly Effective People: Powerful Lessons in Personal Change*. New York: Simon & Schuster, 2004.

they seem earnest? Pay attention in every moment to understand all the different facets of what your customer conveys.

Deepen Your Understanding

You're focused and paying attention, but your mind may still wander as new ideas pop into your head. Unconsciously, your need for acceptance and validation may sneak into the meeting with you, nudging you to add something to the discussion that will win you praise. Instead, focus on how well you understand the other person. Deepen your understanding by asking questions, checking for clarity, and not interrupting.

Even though we're talking about listening, you should feel free to ask questions that will help you better understand what your client is saying. If something is unclear, or you feel like they're holding back, ask questions. You'll be surprised how quickly they open up and how much more you can learn.

Next, consistently clarify! Don't let the conversation roll past you if you don't understand something that has been said. A great way to seek clarity is by summarizing key points and asking if your understanding is in line with theirs. Try saying things like, "Let me check my understanding of this. You want to go forward with a new implementation, but I also sense that such a change may be difficult. Can you share with me more about how you view this change?" Or perhaps you misheard them, or maybe they misspoke and used an incorrect price point. This is the time to clarify.

Finally, except for productive questions for clarification, don't interrupt. You don't need to add anything. It's understandable to want to hear yourself speak, but the truth is that you don't need to talk as much as you feel like you do. And nobody appreciates being interrupted.

Improving your understanding means having a plan to listen more and talk less. Most meetings schedule time for questions, so come prepared with questions to seek understanding. What questions are these? How do you check your understanding? It depends on the type of sales call, but you should generally ask questions that will help you get to know your customer's situation, interests, and needs. When they share their answers, be transparent and authentic in your response. Don't tell someone you agree with them if you don't. Your body language will give you away. Instead, try, "I've never looked at it that way," or "hearing you describe it like that makes me think about this differently." Active listening will deepen your understanding if you take the time to clarify and ask the questions you need.

Beware of Judgment

Finally, remember your mind is so efficient, it's lazy. While someone else is talking, your mind thinks of ways to segment and pattern match their information to your past experiences to make sense of it all quickly. Doing this incorporates the ways you view the world, your politics, your values, and your judgments.

You may not think of yourself as a judgemental person, but you're probably judging more than you're listening. While listening to the other person, check your meta-communication – those words your mind is subconsciously associating with what you're hearing. You need to also watch out for strong emotional responses that make you want to blurt out, "that's not fair" or "that's false." These are all judgments talking inside of you. Your knee-jerk reaction may be 100% correct. However, avoid rushing to a conclusion until you hear and understand the facts. Go into the conversation with an open mind and refrain from assessing intent before you have all the information. Reducing judgment will allow you to focus more fully on your customer.

You should by now understand that active listening requires planning to focus, paying attention, deepening your understanding, and refraining from judgment. Practice these listening skills in all aspects of your life, and soon it'll come as naturally as passive listening. Your customers will appreciate your commitment to them and your relationships will improve.

EMPATHIC LISTENING

The other listening method that you need to practice as a seller is called empathic listening. I learned early in my career that people don't care how much you know until they know how much you care. To be an empathic listener is to understand someone intellectually and also emotionally.

Humans are emotional. Even the most stoic and guarded person feels emotion. Emotion plays a large part in determining human behavior. You need to know how to read the subtext of conversations and listen to the emotions to be an effective seller. When you seek to understand people, use questions to draw them out of their shell, and listen empathically to understand what they are feeling on an emotional level. Understanding their emotions will help you make sense of their actions.

To be an empathic listener, you need to have trust. The other person will not divulge their life's story if they don't trust you. As a boss you might wonder why an employee's performance is slipping, but you can only get to the root of the issue when you earn a degree of trust. Similarly, a salesperson will only understand a customer's needs when they establish trust more deeply. Listening actively and with empathy is the best way to develop this trust.

A common trap that erodes trust quickly is assuming you know someone else's experience. We all want to create common ground and relate to each other, but sometimes these efforts are misplaced. If you don't know what to say, let compassion take the lead and learn to be comfortable with silence.

The ramifications of COVID-19 means you need to listen with empathy now more than ever. The epidemic impacted every person in unique ways. Some people lost jobs, while others lost loved ones. The disease has affected how we work, meet, and play. In 30 years of selling, I've never experienced customers crying on the phone and in video conferences. When you start down a path of empathic listening, it can get real. People want to be heard so much these days, it's almost deafening.

Now that you're thinking empathically, you need to act intentionally. There are three ways you can serve with empathy:

1. On a cognitive level, you seek to understand the other and their experiences.

2. On an emotional level, you desire to understand what the other is feeling and how they deal with their emotion.

3. On a physical level, you put your words to action.

LISTEN TOGETHER

You now have a better appreciation of how difficult listening is, and why it's so important. You know how to practice active listening and empathetic listening. Now it's time to teach your team! Consider implementing "listening training" to prepare your staff and get some extra practice yourself. At important sales meetings, an extra set of ears goes a long way. When the stakes are high, you want to make sure you've listened well and will remember all the vital information. Training your team to practice these styles of listening will ensure you all understand your client perfectly.

After meetings with your team, have everyone review what they heard and understood, and look for opportunities to practice. One of my favorite things to do in sales coaching is to simply observe and listen. While this may seem unnatural at first, extra practice is never a bad thing. Ask to sit in on meetings so you can practice listening and integrating information. Practice makes perfect. When you build a team of active, empathetic listeners, you will all walk away with greater clarity and understanding.

CHAPTER SUMMARY/KEY TAKEAWAYS

In this chapter, you learned:

> **You probably don't listen, but you should**: Sales-people are so focused on what they're going to say next they forget to listen to the customer.

> **We're bad at listening**: Your brain looks for shortcuts and technology decreases your attention span.

> **Active listening**: Active listening involves listening with intent and probing for clarity.

>> **Plan to focus**: Create a distraction-free environment.

>> **Pay attention**: Devote 100% of your attention to what your customer is saying.

>> **Deepen your understanding**: Seek understanding by asking questions when appropriate, clarifying, and not interrupting.

>> **Beware of judgment**: Don't jump to conclusions or let your emotion get the better of you while listening.

> **Empathic listening**: Listen to develop deeper emotional understanding.

> **Listen together**: Teach your team the skills you've learned and bring extra ears to all your meetings.

Now that you understand how to shut up and listen, it's time to learn what you're saying when you're not talking.

WHAT YOU SAY (WHEN YOU'RE NOT TALKING)

What happens in the first few seconds of a meeting can determine its outcome. One morning, Anna woke up late to a burst of anxiety for her big sales meeting. This was her only shot at winning the deal. As she got ready to leave, she realized her new suit was at the dry cleaners and she'd have to wear an older one. She ran out of time to shower and had to do her makeup in the car, but she still stopped by Starbucks and waited in line for her coffee. By the time Anna got to her meeting with Acme Products, she had only three minutes to prepare. As she checked in, she noticed her competitor had signed in an hour earlier to meet with the CEO, Bryce Applebaum. Her confidence wavered as she waited for her meeting.

When she walked into the room she saw Bryce and Sherri, who was in charge of purchasing and was Anna's connection at the company. Anna went to Bryce and outstretched her hand, "Mr. Applebaum, so nice to meet you. My name is Anna Smith, with Epic Solutions." With a smile, Bryce responded, "Nice to meet you, Ms. Smith. You can call me Dr. Applebaum."

Anna froze: she'd forgotten he was a doctor. Then, Sherri left the meeting and in filed a team Anna had never met. After introducing herself, she sat down and pulled out a tangle of cords to set up her laptop. As she fumbled with the projector, she realized she'd already wasted 15 minutes. The authority and conviction vanished from her voice as she began her presentation, and almost everyone in the room was on their phone. Anna made a bad impression before she even started her pitch. She didn't close the sale.

In a sales meeting, even before a word comes out of your mouth, the customer is listening. In the last chapter you learned how to stay quiet and listen to your customers. In this chapter, you'll learn how to communicate positive messages even when you're not talking. First, you'll learn how to control a number of variables in advance to prepare for a good impression. Next, I'll show you how to master nonverbal communication. Finally, we'll touch on how to virtually establish a positive impression through your writing.

WHAT YOU CAN CONTROL

You learned the importance of sales call preparation earlier in this book. Those same principles apply when you're preparing to make an impression with your nonverbals. How you show up is within your control. In this section we're going to talk about what you can control in advance to stack the deck in your favor.

Know Your Location

Learning about the physical environment of the meeting ahead of time is crucial. I recommend driving to the location in advance to get comfortable with the route, parking, and traffic. If you can't physically visit before your meeting, use an online map to research the area.

Here's one of my secrets that may shock my competitors and

customers: I often visit restaurants where I know my competitor and customer will be meeting to observe their style and preparation. I'll arrive early, order breakfast, and quietly watch my competitor prepare for their meeting. In some places it's very easy to gather intel in advance. In Bentonville, Arkansas, where Walmart is head-quartered, it's almost impossible to go to a local hotel bar and not meet others in town for similar meetings. When it came time for me to meet with the RetailLink team members at Walmart, staying in hotels and talking with other vendors gave me an edge I couldn't have gotten on my own.

Know Your Technology

Fumbling with technology is the last thing you want to waste time on. One of my worst sales meetings in my history was due to a lack of communication about WiFi. My entire presentation was WiFi dependent, but the customer's system was too weak to support what I needed.

Ask your customer in advance about their systems. What type of projector will they be using? Do you have the right accessory cord to connect? How fast is their WiFi? Having this information about the room set up and available technology will help you smoothly transition into your presentation and give a competent impression.

Know Your Audience

What do you know about your audience? Have you ever addressed a similar group before? If you haven't, seek out similar groups to network with and practice on.

If you feel intimidated to pitch to a group of experienced doctors, seek out doctors with similar backgrounds in your network who are willing to let you pick their brains. Practicing on a similar audience will give you the background and understanding to confidently approach your meeting. You will distinguish yourself when you show up prepared with topical questions ready for your audience.

Set Your Agenda

Organization is key to making a good impression. When you show up organized, you demonstrate that you are excited about the meeting, well-prepared, and respectful of people's time. The best way to be organized is to construct an agenda and deliver it to all stakeholders and attendees with enough of an advance for them to read it over and submit changes. Sharing an agenda helps people prepare, and engages them more in the content. During the meeting, they may have more insights to share because they had time to think ahead.

In sharing an agenda, you make your meetings more inclusive by giving your attendees the ability to prepare. There are many excellent meeting sample agendas available online. Be prepared, control what you can, and get ready to make a great first impression.

NONVERBAL COMMUNICATION

Now that you know how to take control of the situation before you even arrive, it's time to learn how to improve your nonverbal communication once you step into the room. It's essential to know the nonverbal messages you're sending and how to interpret others' nonverbal behavior. The purpose of communication is to create shared meaning between people, so think about what you're communicating through your facial expressions, physical gestures, outfits, touch, and paralinguistic cues.

Facial Cues

Your facial expression will telegraph your thoughts and help you read the thoughts of others better. One of the most telling places to look when judging another's nonverbal behavior is in their eyes. Dilation of the pupils will often indicate interest or engagement. Looking away may suggest discomfort or boredom. If you notice someone wrinkling their nose or pursing their lips it may express negativity or disagreement.

An excellent way to make a good impression is with a simple smile. It shows you're approachable, open, and is often reciprocated. A smile conveys confidence and is a great icebreaker. Eyebrow arching is another nonverbal expression that signals that you are engaged and kind. Alternatively, scrunched eyebrows suggest feelings of anger and confusion.

Physical Cues

Reading people beyond their faces isn't too difficult. When someone is stressed they may wring their hands, bite their lip, bounce their foot, or touch their face. Be conscious of your body's behavior, as it can be misinterpreted if you aren't careful. For instance, you may be cold, but crossed arms can cause others to perceive you as unapproachable. Crossed arms could be a bad sign in a customer when you're discussing pricing.

Another cue to watch in yourself and your customers is foot alignment. Typically a person's stance will turn away from people they dislike or perceive as a threat, while they will point their feet towards people they trust. In general, nodding signals approval while a shake of the head communicates the opposite. However, constant head nodding, called "non-assertion," is something to beware of in negotiations. Your customer's nods may mean they're brushing you off and aren't interested in developing the relationship any further.

Mirroring is a natural state of synchrony that occurs in genuine communication. When you're in sync with someone, you will unconsciously mirror their gestures and behavior. When this happens naturally it's an excellent clue that you are on the same page. However, I dissuade salespeople from attempting to artificially mirror to manipulate someone into agreement. I know when someone is trying to mirror me and it feels fake and off-putting. Keep your physical gestures genuine and open.

Your Outfit

It's not all about what you do with your body that matters, it's also what you wear. How you present yourself is the first thing your customers will notice. You need to put care into your outfit choices. Whom are you trying to sell to? The answer to this will dictate how you should dress. If you're in a three-piece suit with cufflinks and wingtip shoes selling to any corporation in San Diego, Hawaii, or Miami, you are out of place. You'd have more success in that outfit on Wall Street in the 1980s.

The power of image was on display in the first televised presidential debates between John F. Kennedy and Richard Nixon.[36] Kennedy looked young and well-tanned in a blue suit, which showed up very well on a black-and-white TV. In contrast, the broadcast made Nixon look old and disheveled in a washed-out gray suit. It's a good idea to incorporate a lot of blue into your wardrobe, as it projects trust. Try keeping a record of the clothes you wear for a week and what you think you're communicating with them. Then, at the end of the

---

36   Sidney Kraus, "Winners of the First 1960 Televised Presidential Debate Between Kennedy and Nixon," Journal of Communication 46, no. 4 (1996): xx, doi:10.1111/j.1460-2466.1996.tb01507.x.

week, ask others for their impressions of your outfit choices. How did their feedback align with what you intended?

The phrase "dress for the job you want, not the job you have" is as relevant in sales as in any industry. Take pride in your appearance. Coming from a poor background, it wasn't always possible for me to buy expensive clothes. My father used to tell me "it's okay to be poor, but there's no excuse for being dirty." I've seen people succeed in jeans and a polo shirt because their clothes were clean and pressed and they had great hygiene. Watch what you wear and how you compose yourself. It says a lot about you.

Touch

Physical touch can either make people feel relaxed or scare the hell out of them. It all comes down to context. High-end waitstaff in restaurants know this. Did you know waiters and waitresses who touch their customers gently on the shoulder or arm before leaving the bill receive higher tips than those who don't? Subtle touch can be a useful tool for engaging with your customer and putting them at ease.

Carefully judge the appropriateness of touch in a post-pandemic world. You need to be very cautious about invading personal space. Determine people's openness to close contact before you engage. People are likely to prefer distance these days. Consider asking customers how comfortable they are shaking hands or meeting in a small, enclosed room during COVID-19 and be accommodating of their desires. They'll appreciate it.

Cultural cues also play a role in space and touch. People from the Middle East and Latin America often communicate in closer proximity to each other than Europeans or Americans. Similarly, people in warmer climates tend to touch more. You should also be aware of how gender and sexual orientation will play into the way your touch is received. When in doubt, air on the side of caution to keep everyone comfortable.

Paralinguistic Cues and Nonfluencies

This last aspect of communication combines verbal and nonverbal communication. Paralinguistic cues are the unique ways in which people speak, as opposed to the actual words they are saying. The speed at which people speak, pauses, vocal intonation, and inflections are all examples of paralinguistic cues. Tone can convey a lot about a customer's beliefs and goals. Tonal variance is a great way to engage your customers and make your presentation more exciting. You'd rather listen to someone whose tone mirrors their information than someone with a monotone drone. Be careful with your inflection though.

Have you ever noticed someone ending sentences with increased tonal inflections? This inflection makes statements feel like questions, which signals a lack of confidence. So be careful when you're practicing a speech or presentation to make sure that your paralinguistic patterns are as well crafted as your script.

Beware as well of verbal nonfluencies. These are the "ums" and "ahs" you add without thinking. They also include your nervous coughs and clearing of your throat. Think of them as useless, distracting filler. Nonfluencies detract from the flow of your message and you should cut them out as much as possible.

Hopefully you have a better understanding of all the ways nonverbal communication can help you project a stronger, more confident impression to your customers, as well as cue you into what they may be thinking. The final piece of this chapter will show you how to communicate better in your writing.

VIRTUAL WRITTEN COMMUNICATION

Selling in our modern world means using every communication medium effectively. If you want to get your message across, you need to understand how to be persuasive in person and through mediated means. Virtual written communication doesn't allow you to make a physical impression, so you need to carefully tailor your message to your audience.

Today, the options for writing to your client are not limited to email, but include instant messaging platforms, Facebook, LinkedIn Sales Navigator, Google, Twitter, Microsoft Teams, Slack, various social media sites, blogs posts, text messaging, and more. Our world is oversaturated with these platforms, meaning you have to break through all the noise by choosing the right medium and style of virtual communication for your customer. This section will give you crucial tips for making the most of this type of communication.

When you think of written communication, you probably think about email. It's easy, professional, and quick. These very qualities are also its downfall: I currently have over 60,000 unread emails. In a 2012 study, McKinsey found that email and similar social technologies reduce our productivity by 28 percent.[37] The way these technologies always notify us of "new messages" or "new posts" interrupts our thought processes and distracts us for up to fifteen minutes. We are distracted by the very communication designed to bring us closer together and make us more productive.

With your customers drowning in a sea of messages and information, how do you cut through the clutter and get them to read what you've written? Here are my most useful tips for making your writing effective:

---

37   "The Social Economy: Unlocking Value and Productivity Through Social Technologies," McKinsey & Company, last modified July 1, 2012, https://www.mckinsey.com/industries/technology-media-and-telecommunications/our-insights/the-social-economy.

1. **Grab their attention**: Whether you're writing an email or a blog post, grab your customer's attention with a snappy headline, subject, or title. Your customer probably gets a few hundred emails a day, make sure they'll open yours! Good headlines are clear, concise, drive interest, and inspire action. Here's a lousy headline I see too often: "Just following up." What are they following up on? Why should I even care? Connect your headline to your reader. Some templates for grabbing your customer's attention include: "[Insert name of mutual connection] suggested we talk about [insert problem]" or "Here's how [insert competitor] gained huge benefits" or "Here's a free solution to [insert problem]."

2. **Write in the active voice**: Writing in the active voice makes your writing more concise, engaging, and comprehensible. For instance, "We confirmed product availability" is far better than "Product availability was confirmed by our company." It will fundamentally improve the quality of your writing.

3. **Pick the right medium**: Make sure you've chosen the right method of communication. Does this call for an email? Is a text more appropriate? Does it lend itself to conveyance via your company's social media pages? Is there a better way to communicate your message? If the news is emotional, full of nuance, or prone to misinterpretation, you should probably pick up the phone, schedule a video call, or visit in person. The more prone to ambiguity your message is, the more likely you'll want to choose verbal communication.

4. **Be brief and signpost the next steps**: Be persuasive and brief. Can your email be read in less than 15 seconds? Does

it detail the next steps and spell out clear actions to be taken? Here's an example: "Victoria, Thank you for your time today. We appreciated the information your team shared about the upcoming need to increase your cybersecurity. Our recommended next step is to conduct a security assessment on March 5th. Please confirm that date. Let's also schedule a follow-up meeting for March 10th to review the findings. I'll send a meeting request for both dates. Thanks again, Joe." This is a simple example in 64 words that communicates appreciation and then signposts where you are and where you want to go. Brevity and clarity sell.

5. **Analyze with technology**: Do your emails get read? Do followers engage with your posts? Analytics technology can help you understand if and when your communication is reaching your customers. Email tracking tools like Streak, Yesware, Hubspot, ContactMonkey, SalesHandy, and Mixmax, as well as built-in Gmail and Outlook software, can help you understand if customers are reading, forwarding, or ignoring your emails. Content tracking tools like Seismic, Highspot, Brainshark, and MindTickle are useful as well. With each passing day, new companies and technologies spring up to accelerate sales productivity. Why not take advantage of them and see if your message is getting across?

6. **Proofread your writing**: Virtually all online platforms these days have spell and grammar checking capabilities, so use them. Nothing damages your message more than spelling or grammatical errors. Read and proof all your messages before sending them. Additionally, reread your communications

from the customer's point of view to ensure they are appropriate. The more critical the communication, the more you'll want to have another perspective. Ask coworkers to read over your most important messages. People get fired due to poor communication every day. Adhere to the sunshine rule: everything you write can be exposed in the sunshine. If your message were posted on a billboard for all to see, would you be comfortable? If it would cause you embarrassment or negative consequences, it probably means you shouldn't send it. Adhere to the sunshine rule, and proofread your spelling & grammar!

7. **Use appropriate formality**: Carefully assess the formality of the communication before writing. How should you address the other person? Should you use their first name, last name, title? Judge based on past communications with them or similar individuals and use common sense. If they are listed as Kimberly on their company's staff page, don't fire off a greeting that says, "Hey Kim." Don't mistake the ease and simplicity of virtual messaging for permission to use a casual tone. Wait until you've established a strong relationship first. How you communicate digitally reveals more than you may intend, so go slow, be thoughtful, and empathize with others. When in doubt, air on the side of caution and get a second opinion.

CHAPTER SUMMARY/KEY TAKEAWAYS

In this chapter, you learned:

- **You communicate even when you're not talking**: You're making an impression on your customers even when you're silent. Master nonverbal communication to ensure you always come across well.
- **Control what you can**: Your first impression can be make or break, so prepare heavily in advance to control as many variables as possible.
    - **Know your location**: Research your meeting site in advance.
    - **Know your technology**: Ask your client what technology will be available at the meeting so you can plan accordingly.
    - **Know your audience**: Practice with similar groups before your meeting to exceed your audience's expectations.
    - **Set your agenda**: Create and distribute an agenda well in advance.
- **Nonverbal communication**: Mastering the art of nonverbal communication will allow you to communicate the right message to your customers while interpreting theirs.
    - **Facial cues**: Eye contact, smiles, and arched eyebrows foster trusting and engaging relationships.
    - **Physical cues**: Body language can communicate both cold and open attitudes. Make sure you're giving off the right impression and can read your customer.
    - **Touch**: Touch can be a useful tool for deepening

relationships, but make sure to use it appropriately, especially after COVID-19.

→ **Paralinguistics and nonfluencies**: The pauses, tone, inflection, and "ums" of your speech are important, as well as your speed and nervous coughs. Monitor these and make sure they convey confidence.

➤ **Virtual written communication**: Use virtual mediums like email, instant messaging, and social media effectively by writing catchy headlines, using active voice, choosing your medium wisely, being brief, signposting, utilizing analytics, proofreading, and assessing appropriate formality.

By now you should be a master of all forms of communication. The next chapter will teach you to apply these to forge genuine, lasting connections.

READY, SET, PRESENT!

Despite having an excellent relationship with your customer, a top-notch product, and an unbeatable pricing model, you can still fumble the sale if you don't nail your presentation! Presentations involve sharing ideas to inform, educate, and persuade potential customers. They require a mix of planning, flexibility, confidence, and humility. You must be a confident public speaker to deliver a good presentation, and that's a skill many people are afraid to perfect. Glossophobia, the fear of public speaking, is one of the most common phobias. Presenting can be daunting, but the skills I learned studying Speech Communication will help you get past your fears.

In this chapter, I'll teach you how to nail your presentations. First, I'll walk you through some examples of good and bad presentations. Next we'll talk about planning again, and the specific steps you need to take to plan a stellar presentation. Then, you'll learn how to ace your opening. Finally, I'll show you how to nail your delivery through the art of persuasion and storytelling.

GOOD & BAD PRESENTATIONS

We've all suffered through bad sales presentations. Remember the movie *Tommy Boy*? In the movie, Tommy, played by the late Chris

Farley, tries to save his company by being the best salesman. He embarks on a series of horrible sales calls with no preparation and nearly lights a customer's office on fire. You're probably doing a bit better than that, but there's always room for improvement.

Think of the last lousy presentation you endured. It could have been the weary pitch of a door-to-door seller, the upsell at a carwash, or a tired TV ad. Bad presentations have a distinct feel. Some are rigid and overly scripted, while others are rambling and irrelevant. When planning your presentation, keep in mind the types of pitches you don't respond to, and try not to make any of those same mistakes. Common mistakes of bad presentations include:

> Forgetting the customer's name

> Inappropriate jokes or comments

> Saying "let me be honest" (suggesting you've been lying)

> Nonfluencies (um, ah, so)

> Hard to read PowerPoints (too many bullets, small font, etc.)

> Technological issues

Excellent presentations, on the other hand, are the result of careful planning and preparation. They create a connection with the audience and inspire action. You know you've just witnessed a great presentation when it lingers with you long after you've left the building. Great sales presentations offer creative, actionable solutions. Take a moment to reflect on great presentations you've witnessed and write down a list of what made them so effective. In this next section, you'll learn how to start off strong.

PLAN TO PRESENT

Here it is again, a plan! It should be obvious by now that success doesn't happen overnight. Invest time and effort in planning. Great salespeople make it look easy, but it rarely is. Here are the keys to planning an excellent sales presentation:

1. Define Your Goal

2. Know Your Audience

3. Structure

4. Time It

5. Practice

Define Your Goal

Understanding where you want to end up is where you need to start. Steven Covey's *7 Habits of Highly Effective People* lists "Begin with the End in Mind," as a crucial part of your sales presentation. Understand what you want to achieve in exact detail. Your goals drive your presentation. Think for a minute about your goal. Are you looking to close the sale, or are you looking to earn the right to come back tomorrow? Is your goal to inform or persuade? Do you want a specific person to act? This part is vital. I call this the best possible outcome (BPO).

Your best possible outcome should be something tangible and observable. Ask yourself how you will judge whether your presentation is a success or not. Define the goal in great detail.

Here's an example of a specific BPO: "After the meeting, I will better understand Company X's problem, decision-making process, budget, and timing so we can craft a stellar proposal. At the same time, we will build confidence that our company is uniquely suited to help. We want consensus from the senior executives to meet again within a week."

Know Your Audience

The next step is to understand your audience. Knowing your audience requires time and preparation, albeit in today's modern age, it's not hard to learn about your listeners before your meeting. You can ask peers, associates, or the meeting sponsor for a bit of background, or use social media or your network to find out more information.

It's often helpful to do a trial run with the person who is sponsoring your visit. Receive advice on whether your content is too detailed, not specific enough, or just right. It's the Goldilocks approach to presenting – finding out what is suitable for your particular audience. Ask questions about the audience so you can see things from their perspective. Learn how to make the strongest connection with them.

Think about how to relate to your audience members. What's important to them? Focus your attention on making yourself a valuable commodity to the people you hope to influence. There's a lot of bad advice about how to look around someone's office and size them up quickly. If they have a photo of their family, people tell you to say, "Oh, you have a lovely family. I also have a daughter. How old is yours?" This comes off as inauthentic, not to mention a little creepy. Do your homework ahead of time and develop a thoughtful way to connect instead of sales parlor tricks.

Structure

You know your goal and your audience, now it's time to plug in your talking points and structure your presentation. I suggest you write out the basics before incorporating fancy visuals or presentation tools. Get the bones set first, add details, and then create the slide deck last.

What's the theme or central idea of your presentation? Once you have your goal and central idea, you need to create a series of fundamental points, or "contentions," to back up your vision. Contentions are simply assertions you back up with evidence. Think of your presentation as a stool: you need at least three legs to keep it standing. Presentations usually have three or more contentions. Here's a sample for structuring the body of your presentation:

1. Contention: External companies like ours can help solve problems like these.

    a. Evidence: We have former satisfied customers as references to prove we've successfully done this before.

    b. Evidence: According to experts, external help is critical to solving these types of problems.

2. Contention: We're in a unique position to help you.

    a. Evidence: We have industry certifications.

    b. Evidence: Our particular expertise and processes can solve this faster than the competition can.

3. Contention: Success rests on your engagement.

    a. Evidence: Listen to these testimonials from our most recent customers about their positive experiences.

Include a handful of contentions, and leverage as much evidence as possible. Once you have your contentions and evidence, practice your presentation without any fancy slides. Focus on the clarity and brevity of your message. Like Albert Einstein said, "If you can't explain it simply, you don't understand it well enough."

Timing

Timing is an essential part of your presentation. Just because you have an hour meeting doesn't mean you need to drain all 60 minutes. Less is more. I like to follow the TED rules for presenting by limiting talking time to 18 minutes. Start a meeting with 5-10 minutes of introductions, follow with 18 minutes of presenting, and close with time for discussion. Ideally, you come in under time and nail your main points.

Another technique for encouraging brevity is called PechaKucha, [38]which in Japanese means chit-chat. What distinguishes these presentations is their structure: 20 slides with no more than 20 seconds spent on each, for a total of 400 seconds (just under 7 minutes).

Practice

Practice makes perfect. Any anxiety you have decreases with practice. Once you get past the first 30 seconds, fear reduces by half.

The more unfamiliar you are with the topic, the more preparation you need. Prepare in a quiet place free of distractions. Practice in the same way you'll present, meaning if you will present standing up that's how you should practice. Consider practicing in front of a mirror or video camera to assess body language. Are you making an important point with your hands in your pockets? Watch for anything incongruent between what you say and what you communicate nonverbally. You want your message to come across as strong and consistent.

---

38   PechaKucha 20x20, accessed November 25, 2020, https://www.pechakucha.com/.

Find your voice as you practice. Practicing your introduction repeatedly can help you settle into your rhythm. And how long should you practice? It depends on how well you know your topic. I typically practice 6-8 hours on a topic I am unfamiliar with for a 20-minute presentation.

Once you feel confident, it's time to introduce visual aids. Use aids like PowerPoint to support your key issues, but be careful not to overuse them. Consider your audience. Are people color blind? How well can they see your visual aid? Are you using music or video? If so, how is the sound quality? Will you have a microphone? If so, can everyone hear you? I've been in beautiful board rooms that had sunshine blinding the audience, rendering any aids I was using ineffective. When you do your prep and practice, consider all elements you will be facing.

If you are leveraging technology to assist with your presentation, do a dry run! For instance, most people today are having web-based meetings. It pays to do a dry run on the platform you will be using. Give yourself enough time to react and change plans. Download all the plugins, and make sure your microphone and camera work. No matter how great the technology is, you can always count on last-minute problems arising. Be prepared for the worst. Practice, practice, and practice. You won't regret it.

HOW TO BEGIN

You've planned and practiced, and now it's time to begin! How you start your pitch sets the tone for your entire presentation, so you need to start off strong. The two things I want you to focus on are creating trust and getting your audience to care.

Create trust as soon as possible to earn the right to continue before you make any claims or assertions. Do this by getting the audience to connect with you as a person. Don't start with esoteric abstract ideas or cold data. Connect with your customers. Eye contact is one of the best ways to make sure you connect with your audience. Great speakers switch their eye gaze every 3-5 seconds to make sure everyone feels like they're being spoken to directly. Establish trust by walking your customers through what they can expect from you and fostering a welcoming environment where they are free to ask questions.

Now that they trust you, grab their attention and get them to care. Bill Gates once released a jar of mosquitos on his audience to open a discussion on malaria. Bill said, "there's no reason only poor people should have the experience." He then quickly calmed their fears by explaining that they were not carrying malaria or other diseases. He promptly got his audience's attention.[39]

I once used a similar opening while fundraising. I pulled out a handkerchief and held it up, saying, "a smooth bar of soap, wrapped neatly in a handkerchief and tucked in his breast pocket is all that kept George from losing himself to the streets. Each morning he followed an elaborate ritual of washing, first his hands, then his face and neck." I used gestures to complement my words and visuals of the sink where George washed every day. The audience was riveted and saw the humanity of this homeless man struggling to find work. I connected with them, got them to care, and earned the right to ask for their help and a donation. Brainstorm ways to connect with your customers over your product. Remember, you have to care about what you're selling to get them to care!

---

39   Bill Gates, "Mosquitos, Malaria and Education," TED: Ideas Worth Spreading, accessed November 25, 2020, https://www.ted.com/talks/bill_gates_mosquitos_malaria_and_education.

DELIVERY

You opened strong and forged a connection with your customer. Now it's time to deliver. This final section will cover the art of inspiring your audience and convincing them to buy from *you*. The best way to give a memorable, successful presentation is to use the tools of persuasion and storytelling.

Persuasion

The tools you need to be persuasive are time tested. Aristotle, one of the greatest philosophers of all time, laid out three basic proofs for persuasion in *The Rhetoric*.[40] These tools will help you engage your audience and persuade them to accept your ideas. These proofs have worked since the 300s B.C. and will work in your sales presentation. They are ethos, logos, and pathos:

➤ **Ethos**: This is your credibility. You need to establish credibility before you can persuade your audience of anything. Ethos includes your expertise, knowledge, qualifications, and anything else that makes you an expert on your topic. Fail to establish ethos, and your customers won't take you seriously.

➤ **Logos**: This is how you incorporate reason and logic into your argument. Using data, anecdotes, and other evidence to back up your contentions will improve your logos. Aristotle constructed logical arguments in the form of an enthymeme, a three-part deductive argument consisting of a major premise, a minor premise, and a conclusion. Here's an example: Humans are mortal (major). I am a human (minor).

---

40   Aristotle, John H. Freese, and Ingram Bywater, The Rhetoric and Poetics of Aristotle (Hardcover) (Morrisville: Lulu.com, 2018)

Therefore, I am mortal (conclusion). Craft logical statements like these to incorporate this proof into your presentation.

> **Pathos**: This is your emotional appeal. Move your audience to action by appealing to their emotions. Most boring presentations forget about pathos, making them seem too technical and overly detailed. Pathos helps others make sense of your argument and relate it to themselves. Remember, your customers are human, so play to their sentiments and don't come off as a robot.

Incorporate all three in a natural, balanced way to craft a persuasive presentation.

Storytelling

The other trick I'll share with you is the power of storytelling. Business presentations can get a bit technical and dull. How do you keep your audience's attention and ensure they understand what you're saying? One of the best ways to communicate complexity is to simplify it into a story. Storytelling is a lost art. Many indigenous people, my family included, share information through oral traditions like storytelling. It's an excellent way to communicate a message and keep it interesting.

The stories in your presentations convey complex information while engaging and inspiring your audience. Your stories should support the main points of your presentation and even provide anecdotal evidence. When crafting your stories, remember this rule: Who? What? How? That translates to these three steps:

1. Develop the hero/heroine: This is a company or customer

that your audience will respect and relate to. *(Who)*

2. Explain the problem: What challenges did they have to overcome? These should mirror challenges faced by the customer you are presenting to. *(What)*

3. Present the solution: What action did they take to solve their problem? This is usually hiring your company or purchasing your product. Demonstrate the positive impact your product had. *(How)*

Let's walk through an example. Imagine you're presenting a solution for managing a company's sensitive data. Instead of getting bogged down in technical analysis, you decide to back up your contention that data security is important with a story:

"Let me tell you a story about a modern-day hospital that failed to secure its data." *You've presented a company in a similar industry to them.* "Georgia was the Chief Information Security Officer at the hospital, and one day she discovered her database servers kept resetting as if being controlled." *Start your story with a heroine they can identify with. You're pitching to the Information Security team so they identify with Georgia.*

"She received a demand email, explaining that their servers and data were being held hostage. The hackers demanded a deposit of $6 million in Bitcoin in an offshore account within the next 24 hours, or they threatened to release the records: protected health and financial information of thousands of hospital patients." *You've captured their attention, and now they're thinking about the possible dangers to their data security.*

"The hospital immediately contacted us, and we quickly isolated and expelled the intrusion. Then we worked to swiftly restore and secure the data, preventing the hackers from accessing it. We accomplished this in under 20 hours, so the hospital never had to address the hackers' demands." *You are able to tout the solution your company provided and demonstrate the value of purchasing your technology and hiring your focused team.* "We saved the hospital system 7 years of critical patient records, allowed them to continue caring for patients uninterrupted, and saved them $18 million." *This is the moral of your story and the reason your customer should buy your product right this minute!*

If you want more tips on storytelling, I encourage you to check out an interview with Emma Coats, a former Pixar story artist, who shared 22 tips for a good story![41] Her tips include: keep it interesting, find your ending first, keep refining, and discover why your story needs to be told.

---

41   "Pixar's 22 Rules of Storytelling," The Screenwriting Spark, last modified May 2, 2017, https://www.screen-writingspark.com/pixars-22-rules-of-storytelling/.

CHAPTER SUMMARY/KEY TAKEAWAYS

In this chapter, you learned:

> **Presentations are make or break**: Delivering engaging, persuasive presentations is an art, but you have to master it if you want stellar sales numbers.

> **Good and bad**: The difference between good and bad presentations is planning and practice.

> **Plan to present**: Like everything in sales, you need to have an airtight plan if you want to nail your presentation.

>> **Define your goal**: Start with the end and write down your best possible outcome before you create your presentation.

>> **Know your audience**: Research your audience beforehand to make sure your material is appropriate and relatable.

>> **Structure**: Boil your presentation down to your main contentions and support them with evidence.

>> **Timing**: Keep it short and sweet.

>> **Practice**: Practice until you know your pitch backwards and forwards. Practice your body language and do dry runs of your technology so you're prepared for anything.

> **How to begin**: Start off strong by quickly establishing trust, grabbing your audience's attention, and getting them to care.

> **Delivery**: Put all your practice to work and leave your audience with a memorable performance using persuasion and storytelling.

→ **Persuasion**: Use Aristotle's three proofs to persuade your audience to buy from you: ethos (credibility), logos (logic), and pathos (emotion).

→ **Storytelling**: Communicate complex information and engage your audience's interest by incorporating relevant stories into your presentation.

This chapter taught you how to deliver engaging, persuasive presentations to your customers. The next chapter will walk you through what happens after you've laid all your cards on the table.

WHAT NEXT? STAYING ON TRACK

You can give a stellar presentation and get a verbal commitment from the customer, but if you don't know how to keep control of your sale, you'll risk losing it. Great salespeople always control their sales and work to keep them on track. If you are ever asked, "what comes next?" by a customer, you should be able to quickly and concisely detail next steps for them. This means knowing your implementation timeline, the customer's procurement process, and what needs to be done when.

This chapter will teach you how to keep your sale on track through its final steps. No matter the details of your specific sales process, the final step is usually binary: a yes or no. The first section of this chapter will teach you how to establish where you are in your process and urge your customer to make a commitment. Next, we'll discuss some tips for managing transitions to deliver on your promises. Finally, we'll talk about the importance of following up.

CHECK IN WITH YOUR CUSTOMER

Tools like the Sales Ladder System™ are intended to help you chart a path with your customer and keep you on track to reach your goals. Follow your mutually established process and you'll always know what to do next. Even with your process in place, make sure you're checking in consistently with your customer. Things may change on their end and you want to ensure you're on the same page. Don't be afraid of encouraging your customer to say no. Doing so will reveal areas of misunderstanding or misalignment and provide the opportunity to adjust and realign. To get people to say yes, you also have to be comfortable with them saying no.

At some point in the sales process you must leave it up to the customer to decide how to move forward. Once you've laid your cards on the table it's time for them to decide what to do. Ideally, your customer is sold on your product and you can move to close the deal. If not, here are some common situations and how to approach them:

> **Your customer contact is saying yes to you, but they won't tell you who else is involved in the procurement process**: In this situation it seems like you have a deal, but you've been single-threaded to one contact who is assuming full responsibility for saying yes to you and is refusing to involve anyone else from their company in the process. They are not willing to share who the other stakeholders are and they may try to convince you they are the only one with authority. Be wary of this type of person. They're looking for ego gratification. They want to help you, but may not be giving you accurate information about the process of the sale on their end. There

often is a parallel effort occurring. Maybe the person has personal or positional needs. Getting this surprise solution implemented may help this person and hurt the company. Situations like this are rarely healthy. Strive to get more detail by seeking input from additional stakeholders on the customer side. Ask them questions they may not be able to answer, such as legal questions, or inquire about their value chain, competition, terms, or service management. You will often find this person needs the input and advice of others and does not have the authority to close the deal.

> **Your customer goes silent and misses the date for the next step**: Remember that your customers are people too, and life happens. Be willing to give a little grace. Merely acknowledging the slip and asking for their insight on what happened will often cause them to recommit and possibly explain the reason for the delay. However, after repeated silence the sale is probably in danger. If you have been working openly and honestly, you may already know your customer's decision process or suspect they've been considering a competitor. Let them know the benefits your solution provides over your competitor's. You should also have a robust set of people from whom you can obtain information. Do you have a dialogue with your customer's peers, stakeholders, direct reports, or even their superiors? Seeking input from multiple sources, including administrative assistants, will help you uncover the meaning in their silence.

> **Your customer keeps delaying the goal**: You strive to determine a mutually agreed upon timeline early in the sales process, and you'll want to try to stick to this. It's possible for

plans to change and goals to move. Budgets can be reprioritized, operating structures can be updated, and personnel can change, all of which can cause your process to shift. However, watch out for the constantly moving goal. This customer always changes the outcome and their reasons vary. What once seemed to be a great opportunity now drags on, losing steam. The customer may not have the authority to proceed or may lack the skills needed to get this done. Their financial position may have changed. Whatever the reason, they are stringing you along and your best bet is to approach them directly and ask for a firm commitment either way.

➤ **You examine your process and realize there's nothing left to do but ask for their 'yes or no' commitment**: First, verify that you have received all the commitments you need up to this point. If you realize you haven't, this is a form of no. If you have not received a commitment, you have to go back and restart, which is a painful process and occurs when sellers think they can skip a step to get ahead. If you identify you've received the necessary commitments, it's time to ask them for their decision. Say, "I appreciate all the time and effort we have invested over the last few (days, weeks, months), and understand that we have been in alignment with our values and ideal outcome. Unless there is something else you'd like us to do, I want to ask you for your business. What do we need to do to get started?" If you have invested time and effort, you have earned the right to ask for a commitment to move forward. Be clear, be direct, and be prepared. Ideally, you receive an enthusiastic commitment. But be honest with yourself about the possibility that you may need to walk away from this sale and revisit it when the customer is ready. Keep the door open and reprioritize the opportunity for a future date if needed. Be judicious with your time and know when the moment is right to either close the deal or walk away from it.

MANAGE TRANSITIONS

Suppose you receive a commitment from your customer. Do you know all the next steps needed to get your product's value delivered in the agreed upon time frame? What does every step of the deal look like for all the stakeholders involved? Many sales flounder due to poor execution.

Think of your sale like a relay team on a track. Multiple runners must hand the baton to the other. Each person has a specialty, and while managing each leg of the race is critical to the outcome, the handoff zone is where victory or defeat is decided. Sales is no different. You may have walked your customer through your process flawlessly and earned their business, but when it comes time to transition to the delivery of your solution it falls apart. Failure to manage these transitions leads to customer dissatisfaction, misunderstandings, and even returns or lost sales.

Document both your complete sales process and the customer's next steps in writing, so anyone who takes the baton can easily follow along. Assign responsibility to members of your internal and external teams, with clear expectations on dates and deliverables. Develop a plan for the handoffs. What information is required for a successful handoff? How and when will it occur? How can you make sure this happens effectively? What has worked in the past, and where have you fallen short?

As selling becomes increasingly complex (more regulatory approvals, stakeholders, etc.), a simple mistake can have enormous consequences. Set clear expectations with everyone. If you're delivering a technological solution, make sure you are in touch with your IT and implementation teams throughout the process so they know what the customer expects. You may even consider having support or delivery teams join meetings before they are needed to get familiar with the customer and the delivery expectations. Clear communication and planning are essential to competently managing your transition to product delivery.

FOLLOW UP OR FAIL

John had one of the best sales meetings of his life. The customer, Amy, felt a connection and was sold on the solution immediately. John celebrated his success for days. But as days turned into weeks Amy became increasingly disillusioned and dissatisfied with John. Three weeks passed, and she hadn't heard any follow up from him.

Tired and frustrated, Amy contacted John's competitor and asked them to come in. They were polite and courteous and documented the problem and solution – precisely as John did prior. But before leaving the meeting, the competitor told Amy they would start to work on a plan immediately.

Amy requested a meeting to follow up in a day to assign a resource team. She was clear with her next steps and commitments. So she signed a contract with John's competitor.

John finally called a month later and said, "Amy, it's so great to talk with you again. I've been working diligently with my team, and we are ready to start. All I need now is to get your signature on the contract, and we can be there tomorrow." Frustrated and offended he thought he still had her business, Amy said, "John, I wish I'd heard from you a month ago. I went with another company because

I couldn't wait any longer and felt my business was not important to you."

John thinks back over his mistake. He forgot to send an email summary of the meeting, never detailed next steps, and never sent a thank you card. He set himself up for failure because he didn't follow up.

Don't forget the follow-up. You may have wowed your customer with your presentation and secured a verbal commitment to move forward, but if you don't follow up promptly with meeting summaries, next steps, check-ins, and thank yous, you'll fumble the sale at the last minute.

CHAPTER SUMMARY/KEY TAKEAWAYS

In this chapter, you learned:

➤ **Stay on track**: It's easy to drop the ball on your sales after nailing a presentation. Follow your process closely and check in with your customers to keep the sale moving forward.

➤ **Check in**: No matter where you're at in the process with your customer, check-in regularly to see how you can help move them toward a commitment. When the time comes, be ready to ask them to decide.

➤ **Manage transitions**: Have a plan in place for managing the delivery of your product and make sure team members have clearly defined timelines and expectations.

➤ **Follow up or fail**: Consistently follow up with your clients to ensure they are still on board.

You've learned how to plan your sales calls, nail your presentations, and keep your deals on track. In the next chapter, you'll learn how to close.

CLOSING THE DEAL

The ability to consistently close deals is what separates a stellar salesperson from the rest. If you don't know how to close, you can work hard for months on a sale only to lose it at the last moment. Today's buyers are savvier than ever, and this makes closing harder. Hundreds of techniques for closing exist, but most are woefully outdated. The rapid availability of information has changed selling forever. Customers now have enough information at their fingertips to assess their options before a salesperson even has the chance to close. Sellers also find themselves trying to close accounts involving multiple decision-makers. The average number of people in a B2B sale has increased to eight or more, up from six in recent years.[42] You may even have to close the same person multiple times if your sale drags on for weeks. The sooner you refine your closing technique, the quicker your sales numbers will increase.

In this chapter I'm going to teach you how to close. First, we'll look at some of the reasons you may be holding yourself back from closing. Then, we'll revisit how to sell *with* people. Next, I'll take you through the steps of continuously seeking value alignment along your sales ladder to ensure a final commitment. Finally, we'll cover

---

42   "Top B2B Statistics Every Sales and Marketing Pro Should Know in 2020," Blender, last modified April 15, 2020, https://www.themarketingblender.com/statistics-boost-sales/.

how to hold your customers accountable and see your sale through to the end.

YOU'RE HOLDING YOURSELF BACK

From here on out, I will use the term *close* along with the term *commitment*. For our discussion, consider close and commitment to be synonymous. There are many reasons why salespeople don't like to ask for commitments. However, requesting a commitment from customers is the backbone of your career, and you need to get comfortable doing it. This section will cover some common ways salespeople hold themselves back and will show you how to get past those doubts:

> **Problem #1: You believe it's your job to satisfy the customer.** The customer is always right, so shouldn't your team be as agreeable as possible and strive to create satisfied customers at whatever cost? Actually, no. There is a difference between the sales team and the customer service team. You want to make your customer happy, but you need to know your role. Sales professionals are valued for their insight and experience. Your customers need your expertise, knowledge, and guidance. Your job isn't to pander to the customer. Sellers must stay results-focused. You have an obligation to the growth and health of your business. Countless people depend on you and your sales to sustain the company. You should certainly strive to make your customers happy, but know that at the end of the day your job is to sell.

> **Problem #2: You're worried it's not polite to ask for commitment**. Don't confuse manners with what matters. You can be polite with someone and still disagree. Successful

salespeople often have to persuade their customers to try a new approach or realize the negative impact of inaction on their company. You'll never make the sale if you don't make the ask. You can be professional and polite while still pushing your customer to commit to your solution. Kindness and assertiveness are not mutually exclusive traits.

➤ **Problem #3: You're afraid of 'no.'** Excellent sellers view 'no' as something to seek out! Getting a no provides clarity and helps you identify value misalignment areas or incongruent timing, providing you the opportunity to realign. Remember the Sales Ladder System™: your entire sale is a series of smaller closes designed to help you align value between what you provide and what your customer needs. You've been seeking commitment throughout the sales cycle, don't fear it now. You'll get many nos in your career, including those through-out sales that you eventually turn into big yesses. Don't fear this response. Use it to grow.

➤ **Problem #4: You lack confidence.** In Chapter 1 we unpacked the idea that you need to see yourself as a sales professional. You need to believe in yourself before others will believe in what you're selling. Stop dwelling on negative thoughts like "our price is too high" or "they'll never buy from me." Replace those with affirmations and confidence. Despite all the information at your customer's fingertips, they need your voice now more than ever. Customers are drowning in information, and a confident salesperson can help buyers see the signal in the noise.

Now that you're ready to stop holding yourself back, we'll cover 3 steps for closing the deal.

STEP 1: SELL WITH PEOPLE

The first thing to remember is that selling is not something you do *to* people; it's something you do *with* people. The best sellers establish mutual commitment with customers and help them navigate the buying process simply and efficiently.

My primary beef with popular closing techniques is that many of them involve using trickery or gimmicks to get the customer to do something for you. Rather than learning about the customer, these techniques are about manipulating the customer until they give in. You may close a few deals with these strongarm tactics, but you'll have much more success and better customer relationships when you sell *with* your customers, focus on value alignment, and genuinely try to support them.

In previous chapters, we learned about how buyers make decisions. We also learned that selling with empathy means taking into consideration that you are selling to people who, like you, are imperfect. You develop trust with customers by showing up and helping them when they need it. You'll start closing more deals when you realize that the close is a joint venture between you and the customers. Stop trying to manipulate customers into buying from you.

STEP 2: CONTINUOUSLY SEEK ALIGNMENT

In this section, we'll discuss the next step in closing: seeking continuous alignment. In today's competitive selling environment, you need commitments throughout your sale. When you ensure that you and your customer are aligned throughout the process, closing will come naturally.

Remember the Sales Ladder™ for tracking alignment with your customer? Let's draw it out:

Start by identifying the desired outcome and the relevant timeline for the customer. Place it in the upper left-hand corner. This is the customer's side of the ladder. Once you've established a date and desired end state, you need to help the customer identify important decision points along the way and criteria for making a purchasing decision. It's important to meet your customer where they are. You need to look at the path to the sale from their vantage point and start with a one-sided ladder.

Now for the fun part. It's time to build your side of the ladder by aligning your value and gaining their commitment on each rung of their ladder. Invite your customer to work with you and explore solutions.

Let's say you have a customer who has to reduce their cost of operations and close their data center by December 31st. This is the target outcome and date. Establish that you have an opportunity by assessing if your customer has BANT: the budget, authority, need, and timeline.[43] Let's look at a typical ladder and how to use it to seek alignment and commitment. (This is a broad ladder based on foundational principles; your specific ladder will likely have more detail and potentially more rungs.) We will assume the rungs of the ladder are:

1. Assess application environment and inventory

2. Assess the costs of migration and team required

3. Determine the long term operating environment and costs

43   "IBM | IBM Business Agility | Solution Identification and BANT Conversation Guidelines and Recap Email Formats," IBM HTTP Server, accessed November 9, 2020, https://www-2000.ibm.com/partnerworld/flashmovies/html_bp_013113/html_bp_0

4. Perform the migration and secure the environment

5. Develop new processes and management practices

You now need to align your customer with your value by leading them through the value discovery process. Value alignment involves three important dimensions that you must understand to complete this approach. These dimensions are the glue holding your rungs together. They are all independent but critical to mutual value progression. They are:

> **Internal vs. External**: This is the source of your client's motivation. In the example above, it explains the need for the data center move. Ask questions about why they need to do this to identify whether their motivation comes from an internal factor (such as reducing the costs of operations) or external (such as becoming a more nimble company so they can pursue their growth plans). Understanding the source of their motivation is extremely important for value alignment.

> **Toward vs. Away**: Sales typically happen on a continuum of pleasure versus pain. Companies are rarely motivated to act when things are lukewarm. Rather, it takes success or failure to inspire action. Determine whether your customer is moving toward a goal or away from pain. Are they moving toward more growth and revenues or away from a takeover attempt? Pay attention to their language to determine their reason for the move: "away from" language usually sounds like "we want to avoid spending any more money on this data center" while "towards" language sounds like "we are eager to embark on a new direction." Determine where your customer is on this continuum.

➤ **Aligned vs. Balanced vs. Misaligned**: The third motivational dimension tells you how the customer conceptualizes their value alignment relative to what you are offering. They are either in alignment, out of alignment, or a balance between the two. Seek to move towards alignment one commitment at a time.

Using our example scenario, I will now illustrate how to move towards a commitment from our hypothetical customer by seeking value alignment on the three dimensions as we move up the rungs of the ladder:

1. First, we are going to cater our language of the internal motivation of the company. To gain commitment, we first need to balance the perceived value. Share with the customer, "Assessing your current environment and inventory is critical to understanding the impact this project could have on the company today." Notice the emphasis on internal factors.

2. Next, we are going to share how this helps them move away from a problem. "We have successfully helped many customers like yourself avoid the high costs of continuing operations and the problems that come from maintaining complex systems as they age." Notice the "away from" language. We are moving them away from perceived problems.

3. We also want to move them toward a benefit. You might say, "This has resulted in greater business agility and has the power to transform your entire business, better serve

your customers, and support growth." This utilizes strong "toward" language.

4. You are now going to use language to appeal to the external benefits of accomplishing the desired outcome. You could suggest, "We have a proven process that makes it easy to conduct inventory in a few days."

5. You've ensured value alignment throughout the process and now it's time to gain commitment. You say, "I'd like to explore your ideas to understand what will make this stage of the process productive and valuable. How do you feel about our approach?" Here you are seeking affirmation. Are your values aligned and balanced or out of balance? If you are out of balance, you will hear it now. This will enable you to alter your approach and realign value.

Closing is about gaining commitment to move to the next step in the value chain. Along your path to the close you earn the right to explore possibilities, request the customer's time and resources, and execute your proposed mechanisms to make the outcome a reality. It's important to reaffirm your commitment and value alignment as you move up the ladder.

For instance, when reviewing the process, you might say something like, "over the past 6 weeks, we have come together to assess your data center migration, and we have done a comprehensive assessment that showed you would save about $6 million a year in operational costs and improve key processes. We presented a plan for the migration with costs. For each step so far in the process, we have been in alignment with you, and now we need to gain your commitment with your signed approval to move forward with the migration."

Here it pays to be silent for a second to hear the affirmation. Up to this point, you've provided a clear path forward and aligned value to their outcome. You have discovered areas to be shored up and resolved, addressing each one every step of the way. Your customer will either say yes or no. Follow the ladder, seek alignment, then secure commitment.

STEP 3: HOLD THEM ACCOUNTABLE

You need to get good at holding people accountable to their obligations and anticipating roadblocks. Once you have a customer's commitment, you need a method of helping them own their actions. Create an evaluation plan, similar to a project plan, which details dates and ownership for all remaining tasks. This plan should show the steps in the process of finalizing the sale, when they need to be accomplished, and who is going to be responsible for doing the work.

It's important to get buy-in on each rung of the sales ladder. As you move through your process, display each point visually and seek verbalized commitments. Ask your customer questions like, "Now that you have had a chance to review this plan, are there any changes we need to make to the dates or the ownership?" By seeking clear, verbal affirmation, and accompanying it with written guidance, you are asking for commitment.

Establish a regular time to meet to make sure your sale stays on track and everyone does what they are supposed to do, including your customer. Discuss how any deviations will impact the final date and cost. You can refer back to the Sales Ladder date on the left-hand side and state, "Based on this delay in the process, let's revisit the impact on the overall date here. How have things changed? Is there anything we might do to get this back on track?" It helps to remind them of the value. Think again of moving them toward the solution, away from pain.

When you help your customer and all the stakeholders in the sales process to own and be accountable for their actions, your sale will take on a life of its own. You will be seen as a professional helping them solve problems and move toward desired business outcomes. Your deal should be well in hand.

CHAPTER SUMMARY/KEY TAKEAWAYS

In this chapter, you learned:

> **It all rides on how to close**: It doesn't matter how great a salesperson you are if you can't close deals and ensure firm commitments.

> **Stop holding yourself back**: You are your own biggest barrier to success, and you need to find the confidence to close. Don't be too polite, remember that your job isn't customer service, and don't be afraid of hearing 'no.'

> **Sell with people**: Involve your customers in your process, make sure they feel heard, and sell with empathy.

> **Continuously seek alignment**: Follow your Sales Ladder System™ and seek value alignment at every rung to set a clear path towards the close. Seek to understand where your customer falls on the three key dimensions of value (Internal/External, Toward/Away, Aligned/Balanced/Misaligned) to better understand their motivations and needs in the sales process.

> **Hold them accountable**: Create a process for follow through on the sale after you close and hold everyone involved accountable.

Congrats, you now know how to close! You may be thinking that you can stop reading here, but there's a bit more to learn when it comes to maintaining stellar sales numbers. The next chapter will show you how to amplify your impact.

SECRET #13

AMPLIFY YOUR IMPACT

One of the biggest keys to being great in selling is understanding how to do more with limited resources. There are only so many calls you can make in a day, so how do you achieve more in the same amount of time? The key is to utilize your resources to amplify your impact. You do this by bringing more people into your world, fine-tuning your processes, leveraging technology, and working more effectively. Amplifying your impact means selling when you're sleeping and leveraging all your resources in your favor.

This chapter will teach you how to do that by first covering the importance of establishing mutually beneficial partnerships. Then you'll learn how to amplify your impact by surrounding yourself with supportive board members, advisors, coaches, and mentors. Finally, we'll talk about the importance of utilizing cutting edge technology to get the most out of your sales.

PARTNERSHIPS

One of the best ways to increase your scope and scale is through partnerships. In the context of sales, a partnership is defined as an agreement between multiple parties to work towards a mutual business goal, sharing both the risks and the profits. By partnering with like-minded individuals you can tackle more markets and connect with more clients. This is a great way to quickly improve your efficiency, as long as you follow some guidelines.

What's the Why?

Most companies are looking to grow and expand, and partnerships can make this happen. When you approach a new potential partner, you need to start with the 'why?' Why are you considering working together? What gap in the market are you going to fill together?

Consider the story of Kate Spade, who used to work as a fashion editor for *Mademoiselle* magazine. She noticed a gap in the market for luxury handbags and started a partnership with Andy Spade, who would later become her husband, to meet this need.[44] Her handbags were high quality and affordable enough to become a luxury brand for the everyday woman on the go. Many entrepreneurial partnerships start this way. Hewlett Packard, Microsoft, and Apple all started when people joined forces to create a vision for the future.

Every partnership should start with a why. Why are you partnering and what do you want to create? Starting with your why helps you refine your vision, which is essential to putting your partnership in motion. Your why will be what motivates customers to buy from you and inspires action.[45]

---

44   "Kate Spade," Biography, last modified August 18, 2020, https://www.biography.com/fashion-designer/kate-spade.

45   Simon Sinek, Start with why: How Great Leaders Inspire Everyone to Take Action (London: Penguin, 2011)

Define the Wins

Once you determine your why it's essential to understand what's in it for you and your partner. What is your potential win and what is your partner's? These two wins' are probably vastly different, so don't assume you are each approaching the partnership with the same goals.

I once flipped a house with a partner by putting up the cash outlay for the rehab, while my partner helped show me their process and approach. My win was education, and my partner needed cash. We each benefitted from the arrangement and made more money together than if we would have tried to go it alone.

Partnerships can work at any level as long as you connect and figure out an arrangement that will be mutually beneficial. Maybe your partner needs access to new customers and markets, or perhaps you want to expand into international business and share the opportunity costs. In the end, you have to know what the win is for you and for your partner. Knowing what the other party stands to gain is critical. This is as important as doing a strategic assessment for your own company. You have to know what each partner stands to gain from your time together.

When you win due to a successful partnership, you gain more than you would have alone. Many partnerships last for years, but most have an expiration date, so it's good to understand how to make it work and what to do when it doesn't.

Map the Roles

Every partnership should benefit both parties involved, so when you approach a potential partner you need to understand clearly who is doing what and when. Creating an execution plan to guide your work together is important. Misunderstanding and miscommunication occur when you don't set clear expectations in a partnership. The clearer your objectives are, including KPIs to guide your success, the better the odds will be that a long term partnership can meet the needs of all parties. Your association can be metric-based, time-based, or project outcome-based. It depends on the situation.

Where's the Exit?

A crucial step in partnerships is defining when to end the partnership and anticipating it in advance. It's easy to get caught up in the relationship and believe it will go on forever in the shadow of success. However, every good partnership needs a structure and timeline to inform how long it will last and how it will end. This could take the form of a partnership agreement, a joint venture agreement, a licensing agreement, marketing agreement, or other similar formal plans.

Agree to the conditions of how you will end the partnership to ensure you are protected, and the final intent is clear. I know someone who entered a partnership with no definition and then suddenly passed away. His spouse was now committed to this partnership and had to spend considerable time and money to exit the partnership. Having an agreed-upon exit strategy provides clarity and security.

YOUR BOARD OF DIRECTORS

In sales, you are your own corporation, no matter how many layers you have between you and the CEO. You are on the front lines representing either your own business or your employer's. But you have to learn that no matter how great you think you are, you can't possibly do it all yourself. You have to rely on others to fill your blindspots and invest in your success. This is why I recommend having your own personal "board of directors" to support you throughout the different stages of your career.

When I talk about your metaphorical board of directors, I mean you want people around you who can help you grow. I recommend having someone you respect for their sales expertise, someone with good entrepreneurial talents, and someone with a diverse business background who has seen life through a different lens than you have. It's rare for a seller to have your board of directors convene in a meeting like a typical corporate board does, but it's important to check in with them on a regular basis.

Treat your board members with respect and honor their time. Make your moments with them count. Like your sales calls, have a plan, but be open to their feedback and guidance. Show them you are hungry to learn and reflect their advice back to them. If they recommend you read a certain book, read it, tell them how you applied the information, and then ask for more. If they advised you on how to handle a potential situation, tell them the outcome and evaluate yourself on your own performance. You might say "I followed your advice in the meeting. However, I executed the strategy poorly. It still turned out positively, but next time I want to practice ahead of time so I can have a better outcome." People like it when you are honest about your shortcomings. Your board of directors will change through different stages of your career. Some people will stay for a short time, while others will want to be on your team for the long haul. Now let's look at who should be on your board.

Advisors, Coaches, Mentors

Advisors, coaches, and mentors help you amplify your impact. On the surface, these roles seem to have a lot in common, but they are actually quite distinct and are all necessary to bring your sales to the next level. Let's look at them each in turn:

> **Advisors**: Advisors have specific expertise in areas you want to leverage. You hire them to help you solve a particular problem in an area you don't feel comfortable tackling on your own. Advisors provide introductions, investment, and social proof. Your advisors may help you learn a new skill. Let's say you want to get a job at Google, and you need to understand how they make money advertising. You may want to hire a marketing advisor to teach you about AdWords. Once you've reached your goal, you don't need the advisor anymore. If you are a business owner, you'll want financial advisors, legal advisors, marketing advisors, and many more on call. Advisors hold you accountable and keep you on track to the desired outcome.

> **Coaches**: Your coaches are not in the game with you, but they have played in the past and know what it takes to be successful. Good coaches know how to get great results. They will help you by focusing on your process, habits, and inhibitors. They notice things you may not be consciously aware of. Coaches in business include leadership coaches, sales coaches, negotiation coaches, and many more. Any skill you want to improve through practice and discipline can benefit from a coach. Instead of blundering along and improving through time, trial, and error (which may be costly), you can hire a coach to help show you shortcuts. Coaches also are accountable for helping you get to your goals.

> **Mentors**: Mentorships are natural, supportive relationships. A mentor is someone you look up to for multiple reasons.

When you think about potential mentors, think about people who you admire and want to emulate. You may recall our discussion about starting with big dreams and goals by finding models – people who have been where you want to be and have figured it out. Your mentors are often your models.

LEVERAGE TECHNOLOGY

Technology is a crucial part of amplifying your impact. It allows you to be more efficient, effective, and innovative. Sales in particular has benefited from technological advances. Companies like Salesforce were built to make salespeople more organized and improve their productivity. Sellers can now hold their entire pipeline in the palm of their hand and be productive anywhere, at any hour. Additionally, once your information is digitized, it can be optimized.

What are some ways you may want to optimize your selling data? Well, you can leverage technology to tell you the best way to drive to your appointments. UPS does this to find the best routes for package delivery, and there are applications that can help you chart the best course for your sales appointments. Sales information databases exist to help you find more information about your prospective customers. LinkedIn has taken professional networking to a whole new level. You can find people who you have worked with, people you want to work with, people you admire, and people you want to hire.

Make sure to leverage as much new technology as possible to amplify the impact of your sales. Just consider how quickly everyone moved to virtual meetings due to COVID-19. The top salespeople maintained engaging sales calls, while those slow to adapt fell behind. If you haven't thought about investing in cutting edge technology, now is the time. Artificial intelligence tools, models, and machine learning automation are taking sales by storm. Your competition is probably using it, so you need to keep up or get left behind.

Companies like Affinity, CrunchBase, Clearbit, and ZoomInfo are all rich tools that help accelerate and inform salespeople. (I'm not affiliated with any of these companies and don't benefit financially by recommending them to you.) CrystalKnows provides automated communication coaching based on your customers' personality profiles using advanced algorithms.[46] Tools like DocuSign and Adobe Creative Cloud help with automated forms. RPA, or robotic process automation, help optimize workflow. There are conversational intelligence agents who will help you follow up on leads faster, book meetings, and develop sales practices based on your top performers. You can better analyze why you are winning and losing deals, and automate feedback and coaching. Do you want to break into a global marketplace? Imagine using technology that does real time voice translation via video conference into multiple languages. It's no longer science fiction, it's current technology.

CHAPTER SUMMARY/KEY TAKEAWAYS

In this chapter, you learned:

> **You have limited time and resources**: If you want to succeed in sales, you need to learn to amplify your impact beyond what you can accomplish alone.

> **Partnerships are crucial**: Developing mutually beneficial partnerships will help you expand into new industries and markets and tackle bigger customers. Follow these guidelines to make sure your partnerships are sustainable:

>> **Why**: Understand the motivation of both parties so you're on the same page about outcomes.

>> **Win**: Be clear about what you both hope to get out of this.

>> **Roles**: Set clear execution guidelines so each partner knows their tasks and timeline.

>> **Exit**: Have a predetermined exit plan or end date in mind.

> **Your board**: Boards of directors aren't just for companies, you should have a personal one too. This group can help you stay on track in your goals, and is made up of:

>> **Advisors**: Advisors share their expertise in areas you want to improve.

>> **Coaches**: Coaches help you stay disciplined and refine the best process.

>> **Mentors**: Mentors inspire you and are the models you should emulate.

> **Technology**: Cutting edge technology will help you amplify your impact in ways you could have never

imagined, so stay up to date with the latest innova-tions and leverage them to make your sales game more efficient.

Now you know all the steps of selling and how to leverage a variety of tools to expand your impact beyond your wildest dreams. With all the tools for success, don't let yourself get complacent. This next chapter will remind you to stay curious and constantly look for areas of potential growth.

ALWAYS BE CURIOUS

Curiosity is the difference between becoming complacent when you achieve a moderate level of success versus pushing yourself to new heights. Many salespeople stop learning and growing later in their career, and their numbers plateau. Some are so focused on following their script that they miss key pieces of information about their client that would help them close or expand the deal. These types of sellers live by the conventional ABCs of selling: Always Be Closing.

In this chapter however, I'm going to challenge you to think about this acronym differently. I've found curiosity to be a strong catalyst for action, and believe in sales it pays to Always Be Curious. What does it mean to be curious? The journal *Neuron* defines curiosity as "a drive state for information."[47] When you feed your curiosity, your drive state is piqued, and your body releases dopamine, a feel-good hormone associated with enhanced learning and memory. Being curious may seem simple, but making it a habit in your professional life takes focus.

Curiosity means never settling for the status quo. When you seek to constantly learn, grow, read, discover, and explore you'll get

---

47   Celeste Kidd and Benjamin Y. Hayden, "The Psychology and Neuroscience of Curiosity," Neuron 88, no. 3 (2015): xx, doi:10.1016/j.neuron.2015.09.010.

better results. It requires drive and focus but pays dividends.

This chapter will teach you how to be curious in your professional life. First, you'll learn what curiosity looks like in the sales world. Then, you'll learn how to continuously invest in personal growth. Finally, I'll touch on what to learn.

CURIOSITY IN SALES

Being curious as a seller means not just focusing on your customer and what they want, but actively looking beyond what they say to uncover their latent needs, personal challenges, and unique opportunities. Nurturing an innate curiosity confers a distinct advantage in sales. Organizational behaviorists have identified "openness to experience" as one of "The Big Five" personality traits that make good employees. Openness to experience means being curious, creative, flexible, and imaginative.

As a salesperson, developing your curiosity means being open to learning about your customer and their organization and its people. Genuine curiosity will give you advantages your competition doesn't have. When you seek to understand your customer's situation more deeply, you naturally ask questions that help them open up to you. As you nurture this curiosity and dive deeper into their motivating factors, you'll form a bond based on the information you've shared. When approaching customer meetings, prepare a few appropriate curious questions in advance, but be prepared to improvise because conversations rarely go as planned.

Let's say you find something interesting about your customer's motivations or background but you've already finished your other questions. Don't pack it up and conclude the meeting! Instead say, "I'd really love to hear more about this, how are we doing on time?"

Your customers will sense your real curiosity, and may just grant you answers to questions your competitors didn't think to ask.

Questions are one of the most useful tools in your sales arsenal. Early on, they can be used to gain clarity on a customer's plans. Your questions can help you clarify intent, build alignment and consensus, and refine your value in the solution design or definition stages. Late in the sales cycle during negotiations, curious questions can allow you to define your customer's position and develop solutions. Genuine curiosity can help resolve differences, diffuse situations, and build trust. Get curious about your customers and watch your relationships flourish.

INVEST IN CONTINUOUS GROWTH

We've covered what curiosity looks like in sales, but what does it look like in yourself? Curiosity means investing in yourself. Your personal growth is a never-ending journey. There's always new information to learn, or new skills to perfect. Let your curiosity reveal areas for improvement, and then seek out ways to grow.

Maybe you lack industry knowledge, presentation skills, leadership qualities, negotiation confidence, business writing etiquette, or some other professional skill. In sales, there is always something to learn. I don't care if you are selling cow manure to farmers and think there is nothing left to learn – there is always something. For instance, how does your manure help increase grow time for high yield seeds? What options are there for other fertilizers, and how does your solution compare? What is the role of technology on the farm of the future? All these areas will help you improve your sales, but you need to be curious enough to seek the answers instead of staying complacent with your current success. If you aren't seeing your sales improve, you probably haven't invested enough time and energy in yourself.

As you learn to follow your curiosity and invest in your growth, don't let confirmation bias manipulate you. Confirmation bias happens when you seek out an agreement that your choice was the "right way" of doing things. You'll never foster genuine curiosity when you only read content and listen to people who tell you what you want to hear. Learn about a topic from multiple perspectives to become more informed and lessen your need for confirmation bias. As a salesperson, this will help you construct persuasive approaches. You can't appeal to your customers if you don't know what they are thinking. Learn about both sides and use this information to argue your point of view more persuasively. In sales, this may look like investigating why a customer could choose *not* to go with your solution, so you are prepared to refute them.

WHAT TO LEARN

Hopefully you're ready to invest in yourself and let your curiosity guide your sales, but you may be wondering "what should I learn?" There's not one right answer to this, but as a general rule you should focus on things that will improve your professional toolkits, challenge you to think differently, or are simply fascinating to you. How you gather this information is up to you, but I recommend developing a voracious appetite for reading.

CEOs of Fortune 500 companies read on average 1-2 books a month, minimum. Whether you are early in your career or a senior executive, you can always learn from others and gain new insights. If books are not your thing, try audiobooks. I had a 2.5 hour commute each day and in the course of a year I was able to read' over 30 audiobooks. It was much better than listening to the radio and I learned many valuable skills. Or maybe you are a podcast person or like you watch videos. However you prefer to learn, the information age has you covered. It's never been easier to learn anything you want in your free time. You can pick up a new language, take free classes online, or simply read a chapter each night. You're never too old or too young to learn. Let your curiosity drive you.

CHAPTER SUMMARY/KEY TAKEAWAYS

In this chapter, you learned:

> **Without curiosity, you will stagnate**: Always Be Curious should be your professional and personal motto in order to make sure you keep growing and improving.

> **Sales require curiosity**: Approach customers with a genuinely curious mindset, ask lots of questions, and watch them open up to you.

> **Keep growing**: Let curiosity drive you to invest in yourself, and seek out conflicting perspectives to fight confirmation bias.

> **What to learn**: Educate yourself about what interests you and what will help you grow both personally and professionally. There's a range of educational mediums to choose from, so find what fits and stay curious.

Your newfound curiosity will push you to greater heights. In the final chapter, we'll talk about what to do when you reach those heights: how to handle success.

HANDLING SUCCESS

If you follow the secrets I've shared in this book, I'm confident you will reach new levels of success. But sometimes it can be hard to handle a new lifestyle when you rocket to the top so quickly. It happens all the time with pro athletes who don't know how to budget their money and end up wasting millions and declaring bankruptcy. When you find success thrust upon you it's easy to get caught up in all the glamour and develop unsustainable habits. This final chapter will impart a bit of wisdom about how to handle your success. I'll first talk about how to live like a rockstar, then we'll discuss the importance of charity, and finally, we'll cover your walkaway fund.

LIVING LIKE A ROCKSTAR

If you stick with selling, you'll probably go through a phase where you are simply on fire. Maybe you've landed a sales job for a hot company or the marketplace is primed for what you are selling. This section covers what to do when you are successful. I'm talking about success beyond your wildest expectations, the kind where you simply feel like you can do no wrong, and the money keeps flowing your way.

First of all, when and if this happens, give thanks. Give thanks every day. You're going to want to start buying things you think you need: a new car, a new house, etc. There is nothing wrong with this. It's what I call the "Rockstar Life," and it's enjoyable while it lasts, but you need to expect it to stop someday. It can be incredibly hard to slow down your life when the money slows down. That's why I'm telling you to resist the urge to fully give in to this lifestyle. Try to live like you're broke instead.

To cope with success, you need to reexamine your understanding of wealth. Adopt an abundance mentality instead of a poverty mentality. The poverty mentality is the belief that no matter what you do, you will never have enough, that life is a never-ending struggle. When you are poor, you covet what everyone else has. In the end, you believe your failures are all your fault and feel the stars are aligned against you.

The poverty mentality is a trap and it's essential to understand the impact it can have on all areas of your life. How does it affect your decisions? Do you feel there is never enough? That you will always struggle?

I know first hand the struggles of poverty. My father left when I was eight years old and I became the man of the house. We had an acre and a half of land and I took responsibility for mowing the yard every week. My sister cooked us dinner while my mother worked in the front of our house, cutting hair. We chained our dog to the gas meter so the meter man couldn't get a reading on it and we could delay being shut off for another month. Having power, gas, and water was a luxury.

This experience put a chip on my shoulder. I saw others who had more, and I wanted what they had. Poverty mentality keeps you down and keeps your dreams on ice. I've shared my struggles hoping that some of you can relate and understand how this mentality may control your lives. Especially now, with the COVID-19 pandemic, many sellers have lost their jobs and livelihoods, and have been left wondering what comes next.

Flipping the switch from a poverty mentality to an abundance mindset is hard but essential. As you grow in your sales career, you have to change your relationship with success. Abundance means there will always be enough. It is the direct opposite of poverty. Successful people believe there is abundance all around. They don't see or sense scarcity – they live in abundance and expect more of it. And guess what? An abundance mentality returns abundantly.

When you stop thinking about limits and start thinking success, the odds change. Here's an example: what happens when you hit your sales quota? You are on cloud nine, have a spring in your step, probably still have time to do more. You make that next call, unencumbered by limits or nerves. And guess what? You make another sale, and another, and another. Pretty soon, you are closing in on 200%. You start telling yourself you are unstoppable and you begin to believe it. Changing your expectations is powerful and opens you up to new possibilities. To start living like a rockstar, change your mindset.

LEAVING A LEGACY

While it may seem natural to hoard your money and save it for the future, you need to instead focus on giving. Giving is essential to growing as a person. Believe it or not, when you give to others you receive more in return. It may seem trite to say so if you haven't experienced it for yourself, but it's true.

Giving creates muscles of gratitude that grow as you use them. There are so many beautiful ways to give of yourself, your time, and your money. Even the Bible admonishes believers to share their firstfruits – the top portion of their earnings. You may be thinking it's foolish to give part of what you earn to others, but it is not. It's humbling and fulfilling. It completes you in ways you never dreamt of.

There are countless ways to give. Give financially to charities, hospitals, food banks, schools, and homeless shelters. Ask how you can provide, and you will learn of millions of new ways. Another great option is to give your talents. As you grow and develop selling skills, offer to utilize these skills to help charities fundraise. When you feel as though the world has kicked you in the teeth, go and give your time to help another person. You will find that when you give of yourself, the benefits you receive will uplift you in ways a paycheck cannot.

YOUR WALKAWAY FUND

The final piece of advice I will impart is this: establish a walkaway fund. This means having enough money in your bank account to simply walk away when the time comes. In case you ever find yourself working under a toxic manager, you'll want the financial security to just leave.

Too many people don't have the luxury to say, in the words of country-western singer Johnny Paycheck, "Take this job and shove it!" Too many people live by the poverty mentality and don't keep any reserves. I recommend you keep a year's salary in some sort of investment fund – that way, it's working for you while you are working. Invest in stocks, bonds, index funds, gold, bitcoin, real estate, art, land, or cattle. Having enough money to walk away gives you confidence and security and helps you sell.

When you know you can provide for yourself and family while still walking away from a bad situation, you'll feel more relaxed about meeting your customer's needs. You won't be worrying about the next paycheck. In time, you will find you are more concerned about how you're going to give your money away.

CHAPTER SUMMARY/KEY TAKEAWAYS

In this chapter, you learned:

> **Being successful comes with its challenges**: If you work hard in sales you can achieve success beyond your wildest dreams, but it may be more difficult to manage than you anticipated.

> **How to live like a rockstar**: It's okay to indulge a bit when you make it big, but make sure to give thanks and do yourself a favor by living from an abundance mentality rather than a poverty mindset.

> **Leave a legacy**: Giving is more rewarding than getting. Make it a practice to give generously of your money, time, and talents, and you'll lead a more fulfilling life.

> **Establish a walkaway fund**: Start saving early so you'll have the financial security to provide for your family and walk away when the time is right.

You have the tools to make it big, and you know how to handle your success as well! The final section of this book, the epilogue, will recap what you've learned and leave you with my key takeaways to help you chart your own billion dollar sales journey.

Congratulations, you've made it through *Billion Dollar Sales Secrets*! Hopefully, you feel more confident to go out and conquer massive sales with the lessons and tools you've learned in this book. These secrets you've learned will stay relevant throughout your career, no matter what stage you're at. Novice salespeople and seasoned veterans alike can always use a bit of help, and this book can serve as a guide whether you're just starting out or at the height of your career. Before I wrap things up, let's summarize once more where we've been.

CHAPTER SUMMARIES

Secret #1: Look Inside

You are your own biggest obstacle to success! Confront your pre-existing biases, find your unique brand, set your personal and professional intentions, and develop healthy habits to help you succeed. Look inside with a critical eye to understand your strengths and weaknesses and learn how you may be holding yourself back.

Secret #2: The Yin and Yang of Rapport

Building meaningful rapport with your customers should be your first priority in sales. Follow my Greet-Relate-Question-Reflect formula to form genuine connections with your customers, but remember to stay flexible and adapt to unique situations as they arise. Take action to initiate relationships and you'll be building successful connections with customers before you know it.

Secret #3: Rise Up

You'll never achieve the success you dream of if you let your fear hold you back. You have to rise up and conquer it! Develop these traits to help you persevere even when you don't think you can: a positive attitude, empathy, resiliency, authenticity, passion, confidence, focus, and discipline. You'll have days when you don't feel like getting up, but what sets superstar salespeople apart is their ability to push through!

Secret #4: It Takes a Plan

You are nothing without a solid plan. Take the time to prepare because you *can't* wing it. Start with a bold dream, then craft a detailed plan. Prepare for everything you can: sales calls, opportunities, presentations, etc. Follow through on your plan using a process, either the classic Sales Funnel approach or my Sales Ladder System™. Make sure to analyze and track your progress throughout the process to stay on track with your plan.

Secret #5: High-Quality Connections

Sales is a people-oriented business, which makes selling tricky because people are inherently unpredictable. Manage your interactions with customers by studying human behavior and building trust. Choose the right medium for connecting with your customers to overcome common barriers to communication. Finally, look at what's below the waterline to connect on a deeper level with your customer.

Secret #6: What Do You Bring to the Party?

You have to know how you present yourself to others in order to be an effective salesperson. Make the best possible impression by preparing the perfect image, utilizing storytelling, considering the six people in every interaction, leveraging pre-communication, and perfecting your brand.

Secret #7: Sales Managers Suck

Your professional relationships will either bolster your career or hinder it. Even if you think you have the worst sales manager in the world, it's time to stop making excuses and be the bigger person. Follow the approaches in this chapter to handle a variety of difficult managers. If you are a sales manager yourself, be the best manager you can be by showing understanding and compassion, making your vision contagious, modeling a competitive spirit and strong integrity, showing your employees appreciation, and being authentic. Regardless of your position, make sure you are constantly expanding and developing your professional network. You never know when a LinkedIn connection could turn into your dream job!

Secret #8: Listen Up

You probably have a variety of bad listening habits to kick, so stop talking and start listening!   Engage in active listening   by focusing, paying attention, seeking understanding, and suspending judgment. Practicing empathetic listening will deepen your emotional connection with your customers. Listening is a team sport, so train your colleagues to listen well and bring extra ears to meetings.

Secret #9: What You Say (When You're Not Talking)

Once you're listening better, focus on what you communicate to customers even when you aren't talking. Your first impression is crucial. Make sure it's a good one by researching meeting locations in advance, knowing your technology well, preparing for your audience, and setting an agenda. Master nonverbal communication by controlling your facial and physical cues, appropriately incorporating touch, studying your unique paralinguistic tendencies, and watching for verbal nonfluencies. Use virtual communication effectively and appropriately in the digital age.

Secret #10: Ready, Set, Present!

Presentations are the backbone of your career as a salesperson. The difference between exceptional and lackluster presentations is planning and practice. Plan your presentations using the tools discussed in Chapter 4: defining a clear goal, knowing your audience, structuring your presentations clearly and logically, keeping it short and sweet, and practicing, practicing, practicing! Start off your presentations by grabbing your audience's attention and quickly establishing trust. Deliver your talk with confidence using the tools of persuasion: ethos, logos, and pathos. Communicate complex information through engaging stories.

Secret #11: What Next? Staying On Track

Keep your sale on track after nailing your presentation by checking in with your customer to see how likely they are to commit. Manage the transition between your team and the delivery and implementation teams. Then quickly follow up with your customer.

Secret #12: Closing the Deal

If you aren't closing deals it's because you're holding yourself back! Don't be afraid to ask for commitment. Sell *with* your customer, not *to* them. Move your sale through its process by continuously seeking alignment with your customer and understanding their motivations along with the Internal/External, Toward/Away, Aligned/Balanced/Misaligned dimensions. You'll easily close the deal if you've maintained value alignment throughout the sales cycle. Hold your customer accountable to their commitment with an evaluation plan and regular check-ins.

Secret #13: Amplify Your Impact

You're only one person, so if you want to take your sales numbers to the next level you need to learn to amplify your impact. Do this by engaging in mutually-beneficial partnerships, surrounding yourself with supportive advisors, coaches, and mentors, and leveraging cutting edge technology to make your work more efficient.

Secret #14: Always Be Curious

The ABCs of sales is Always Be Curious! This book has talked a lot about introspection and self-motivation for personal growth. This chapter reminds you that to excel in sales you need to approach your customers with genuine curiosity, invest in your continual improvement, and nurture a voracious appetite for knowledge.

Secret #15: Handling Success

If you apply these secrets, you'll reach sales numbers you never dreamed of. To handle that success you'll need to adopt an abundance mentality instead of a poverty mentality, learn to give generously, and establish a walkaway fund as soon as possible.

BIG TAKEAWAYS

I hope you feel like you've learned a lot! I'll leave you with five final key takeaways. If you remember nothing else, remember these five points:

> You are your own biggest hurdle to success. Know yourself and invest in personal improvement.

> Be curious, listen more, and talk less. Then take what you've heard and use it to grow.

> Genuinely connect with your customers and build meaningful rapport before you even think about selling.

> Sell *with* customers, not *to* them.

> Plan, plan, plan... then practice!

You put in time and effort to read this book and now you're equipped with some of the best sales tools in the business! Work hard and trust yourself. I wish you luck in your career. Remember luck favors the prepared. I hope every one of you starts seeing the record sales numbers you've been chasing. If you're interested in continuing your sales education with free downloads, courses, and other awesome resources, head over to billiondollarsalessecrets.com. Best of luck chasing your next superstar sale!

ACKNOWLEDGMENTS

So many people have helped make this book a reality. It started more than three years ago, and I worked at many different moments, writing on my way to work, while I was selling and managing a sales team. I also finished up my MBA while I was writing. Most importantly, I was watching my girls grow into lovely young ladies.

Thanks to my wife and family, who in the middle of work, classes, and life, allowed me time and space to write and encouraged me every step of the way.

To Jamie, your coaching and insights make me a better person. Your friendship during this process meant more than you know. You always reignited positivity in me.

To Andy Earle, I appreciate your thoughtful approach to helping me fine-tune my voice, and making this book come alive.

To George Stevens, thanks for capturing the spirit of this book in your art and design.

Thanks, Brain.fm. Your content helped me stay focused on the goal.

Since this is my first book, I want to write more. Please take time to leave a review for me. Reviews help others and may even help me get a literary agent for my next book. It also makes all that time and effort spent seem worth it as well. Thanks

NOTES

NOTES

Made in the USA
Coppell, TX
30 April 2021